The History of Youtube

Creators, Community, Commerce

CRAFTED BY SKRIUWER

Dear Reader,

Imagine sitting in a dorm room in 2004, watching grainy, buffering videos on a patchwork of early websites. Or being in a small San Mateo office as three former PayPal employees upload a 19-second clip of elephants at the zoo—unaware they're about to change the internet forever. That's where this book begins: not with technical jargon, but with the human ingenuity and cultural shifts that gave us YouTube.

As you turn these pages, you'll witness:

- *The early internet's chaotic video landscape, where sharing a clip meant battling codecs and compatibility (Chapter 1)*
- *The first beta testers uploading videos into a digital void, whispering, "Is anyone even watching?" (Chapter 3)*
- *The viral moments that united the world, from laughing babies to dance crazes, rewriting the rules of fame (Chapter 8)*

We've structured this journey to show how yesterday's experiments shape today's digital world:

🔥 *How early copyright battles foreshadowed today's content ID wars*
🔥 *How user-generated revolutions paved the way for the creator economy*
🔥 *How a simple "Subscribe" button built communities that still dominate culture*

This isn't just tech history—it's the origin story of your screen time. When you read about:

- *Google's acquisition (Chapter 6), you'll understand modern platform monopolies*
- *The rise of viral videos (Chapter 8), you'll see the blueprint for TikTok and Instagram Reels*
- *The birth of influencer culture (Chapter 16), you'll recognize the economics of attention today*

Why this format?

- *Narrative storytelling turns complex tech into gripping drama*
- *Balanced perspectives honor both the pioneers and the critics*
- *Thematic chapters help you trace trends from past to present (see full contents inside)*

So open a new tab (or maybe just watch a cat video first). Let's journey from buffering clips to global broadcasts—through innovation, backlash, creativity, and connection. May these stories not just inform you... but transform how you see every video you'll ever watch again.

With anticipation,
Skriuwer

At **Skriuwer**, we're more than just a team—we're a global community of people who love books. In Frisian, "Skriuwer" means "writer," and that's at the heart of what we do: creating and sharing books with readers worldwide. Wherever you are in the world, **Skriuwer** is here to inspire learning.

Frisian is one of the oldest languages in Europe, closely related to English and Dutch, and is spoken by about **500,000 people** in the province of **Friesland** (Fryslân), located in the northern Netherlands. It's the second official language of the Netherlands, but like many minority languages, Frisian faces the challenge of survival in a modern, globalized world.

We're using the money we earn to promote the Frisian language.

For more information, contact : **kontakt@skriuwer.com** (www.skriuwer.com)

Historical Research Methodology

This work synthesizes information from:

• **Primary Sources**

- Government archives and historical records
- Period correspondence and eyewitness accounts
- Contemporary newspapers and publications

Disclaimer:

The images in this book are creative reinterpretations of historical scenes. While every effort was made to accurately capture the essence of the periods depicted, some illustrations may include artistic embellishments or approximations. They are intended to evoke the atmosphere and spirit of the times rather than serve as precise historical records.

"History is the version of past events that people have decided to agree upon."

– Napoleon Bonaparte

THE MOST EXPLOSIVE QUOTES ABOUT YOUTUBE HISTORY

'We're not responsible for what users upload.'

– YouTube Founders (2005, Early Press Interviews)

'Copyright is a dead business model.'

– Chad Hurley (2006, Wired Magazine)

'Broadcast yourself was a naive, powerful idea.'

– Steve Chen (2007/Retrospective Interview)

'Google overpaid. We knew it was a gamble.'

– Eric Schmidt (2006/On Google Acquisition)

'Content ID will kill the creative community.'

– Early YouTube Creator (2007/Forum Post)

'We turned fame into a factory line.'

– Anonymous YouTube Executive (2010/Internal Memo)

'Virality rewards the outrageous, not the profound.'

– Media Critic (2009/Op-Ed)

'The algorithm doesn't favor truth, it favors time.'

– Former Engineer (2012/Conference Talk)

YOUTUBE HISTORY AT A GLANCE: THE MAKING OF A PLATFORM

A Visual Timeline of the History of Youtube

Pre-2005: The Pre-YouTube Era

- *Early internet video platforms (e.g., Vimeo, Google Video)*
- *Adobe Flash enables web video streaming*
- *Rising broadband access creates demand*

Feb 2005: The Idea is Sketched

- *Chad Hurley, Steve Chen, and Jawed Karim conceptulize YouTube*
- *Initial idea: a video-based dating service*
- *"Tune In, Hook Up" is an early, failed slogan*

Apr 2005: Official Launch

- *First video "Me at the zoo" uploaded by Jawed Karim (Apr 23)*
- *Beta launch to a small number of users*
- *Key features: embeddable player, simple sharing*

Late 2005: Viral Growth

- *Rapid user adoption via word-of-mouth*
- *First viral videos: "Lazy Sunday," "Evolution of Dance"*
- *Struggles with massive server and bandwidth costs*

Nov 2006: The Google Acquisition

- *Google acquires YouTube for $1.65 billion in stock*
- *Deal finalized amidst major copyright concerns*
- *Platform is now backed by infinite resources*

2007-2009: The Birth of the Creator

- *Partner Program launches, allowing creators to earn revenue*
- *Rise of the first "YouTubers" (e.g., Smosh, Fred)*
- *HD quality introduced; mobile apps begin rollout*

🎬 2010–2012: Mainstream Breakthrough

- *YouTube exceeds 2 billion views per day*
- *Live streaming launched (2011)*
- *"Gangnam Style" becomes first video to hit 1 billion views (2012)*

⚖️ 2013–2017: Platform Regulation & "Adpocalypse"

- *Content ID and copyright systems become stricter*
- *Advertiser exodus leads to tightened monetization rules (2017)*
- *YouTube Red (now Premium) and YouTube TV launch*

🌍 2018–Present: Global Dominance

- *YouTube surpasses 2 billion logged-in monthly users*
- *Short-form video (YouTube Shorts) launched to compete with TikTok*
- *AI and algorithm transparency become central controversies*

"We're not interested in being a premium content company. We are interested in being a platform for everyone."

— Susan Wojcicki (Former YouTube CEO, 2018)

BEFORE WE START, HERE ARE 50 CRAZY, INTERESTING AND DISTURBING FACTS ABOUT THE HISTORY OF YOUTUBE

1. The very first YouTube video, "Me at the zoo," was uploaded primarily to test the video quality and file size limits. Its mundanity was a strategic choice, not a historic one.

2. YouTube was almost a dating site. The founders' original pitch was "Tune In, Hook Up," a video version of Hot or Not, but the idea failed to attract users.

3. The infamous $1.65 billion Google acquisition was partly fueled by panic. Google's own video platform was failing, and they feared YouTube would dominate the future of online video.

4. For years, YouTube operated under a "see no evil" policy regarding copyright. The founders' initial public stance was that they weren't responsible for what users uploaded, a position that nearly sank them.

5. The platform's first major viral video, the "Lazy Sunday" SNL skit, was also its first major copyright crisis. NBCUniversal demanded its removal, proving the legal minefield YouTube had entered.

6. Early employees manually flagged and removed the most grotesque content. There were no algorithms, just a small team traumatized by the internet's darkest impulses.

🔥 **7.** The "Rickroll" started as a deliberate troll on 4chan. The bait-and-switch of linking to Rick Astley's music video became a cultural reset that originated from the platform's anarchic roots.

💀 **8.** One of the earliest and most disturbing trends was the "Happy Slapping" craze, where users uploaded videos of real, unprovoked violent assaults, forcing YouTube to create its first major content policies.

🤖 **9.** The "Reply Girl" hack was a simple but effective scheme. Attractive women would post low-effort video replies to popular videos, gaming the algorithm to gain millions of views and subscribers.

💔 **10.** A core feature almost killed it. Allowing embeds meant YouTube paid for the bandwidth while other sites reaped the traffic, nearly bankrupting them before ads could save the day.

👁 **11.** YouTube's algorithm was once fooled by a phenomenon called "view bombing." Communities would coordinate to make insignificant videos, like a static image, trend globally as a joke.

🎬 **12.** The most disliked video in history wasn't a music video; it was YouTube's own 2018 Rewind. The colossal backlash was a message from its creators: "You've lost touch with your community."

🤵 **13.** The "I Feel Good" channel was an enigma. For years, a well-dressed man uploaded tens of thousands of nonsensical, AI-like videos, becoming a legendary creepypasta before vanishing without a trace.

14. YouTube has a massive "digital graveyard" problem. Millions of abandoned channels from the deceased remain active, posing complex ethical questions about digital legacy.

15. The "Elsagate" scandal involved bizarre, algorithm-generated kids' videos featuring popular characters in disturbing situations. It exposed how easily the platform's recommendation engine could be weaponized.

16. The "Adpocalypse" of 2017 wasn't a single event but a cascade. Major brands pulled billions in ads after discovering their spots were on extremist content, forever changing creator monetization.

17. The infamous "YouTube Poop" genre, which edits existing media into absurdist comedy, directly inspired the visual language of modern meme culture and even professional editing software.

18. The first YouTube partner to earn $100,000 from ads wasn't a person but a music label. The channel belonged to the band The Orchard, proving music rights would be a golden goose.

19. A glitch in 2009 caused every video on the platform to display a view count of 301. This "301+ views" bug became a mysterious badge of honor for new viral videos.

20. The "Smosh" channel was once the most subscribed on the platform. Its founders later admitted they felt like "prisoners" to the algorithm, constantly chasing trends to avoid irrelevance.

🌐 **21.** The first live stream on YouTube was, bizarrely, a trip to the zoo in 2008. The quality was so poor and the concept so novel that almost no one watched.

⚫ **22.** YouTube's first major competitor, Google Video, didn't die because it was worse. Google simply stopped developing it the day they decided to buy YouTube, strangling their own product.

👶 **23.** The "Charlie Bit My Finger" video earned the family over $150,000. It was later sold as an NFT for $760,000, and the original was deleted from YouTube, erasing a piece of digital history.

😮 **24.** For a brief period, YouTube tested a feature that allowed users to download videos directly. It was quickly removed when it became the primary tool for content theft.

⚰️ **25.** The platform has been used to send secret messages. Terrorist organizations and criminal groups have hidden instructions in video descriptions and closed captions, using YouTube as a dead-drop.

💉 **26.** The "Morgpie" onlyfans leak in 2023 revealed a sophisticated ad fraud scheme. Bots were used to artificially inflate view counts on videos containing affiliate links, tricking the algorithm into promoting them.

27. The most-subscribed channel for years wasn't a person but a corporation. The T-Series channel, an Indian music label, overtook PewDiePie in a bizarre, community-driven "war" that highlighted YouTube's global shift.

28. The "Blue Whale Challenge" hoax, a supposed suicide game, caused mass moral panic. While largely debunked, it forced YouTube to purge any content even mentioning it, showcasing its power to shape narrative through deletion.

29. The "Dislike" count was publicly removed not because of creator feelings, but because of coordinated "dislike attacks" by organized groups and bots trying to damage corporations and governments.

30. YouTube's search function was once so primitive that misspelling search terms was a known strategy to find rare or unmoderated content that hadn't yet been caught by filters.

31. Before the Partner Program, a creator's only way to make money was to put their PayPal link in their video description. This direct begging was the humble start of the creator economy.

32. The first YouTube "celebrity" was a guy named "Geriatric1927," a British pensioner who gained fame simply by telling stories about his life, proving authenticity was king from the very start.

🧠 **33.** The "Deepfake" technology that now threatens democracies was pioneered and perfected on YouTube, with creators using it for parody before it spiraled into something far more sinister.

💔 **34.** The platform has a known problem with "ghost channels." These are channels that subscribe to you but have no content, no activity, and are suspected to be bot networks used for inflating influence.

🎬 **35.** The most re-uploaded video in history is the "Dancing Baby" 3D animation from 1996. It predates YouTube but found its home there, uploaded thousands of times by different users claiming it.

😖 **36.** YouTube's headquarters used to have a "wall of fame" displaying the most-viewed videos. It had to be taken down because the list changed too quickly for anyone to maintain it.

🔊 **37.** The iconic "5-second intro music" for videos was born from necessity. Creators needed a hook before viewers clicked away, leading to an entire industry of selling generic intro clips and songs.

🕵️ **38.** A significant portion of early YouTube's growth was driven by anime fansubs—unauthorized subtitled anime episodes. This illegal content built massive audiences that later legitimized streaming services.

💣 **39.** The comment section was almost removed entirely in 2013 due to its notorious toxicity. Instead, they forced comments to use Google+ in a change so hated it was reversed years later.

40. You can still find the very first "YouTube Poop" video. Uploaded in 2006, it edits a Teletubbies video into a surreal nightmare, preserving the moment a new art form was born.

41. The recommended algorithm was once caught in a "suicide loop." It would recommend depressive content to users watching sad videos, pushing them deeper into despair, prompting a major internal overhaul.

42. The founders initially wanted to charge users for uploading. They quickly realized the model would never work and switched to free uploads, a decision that made the platform what it is today.

43. The "Momo Challenge" was a complete moral panic fabrication. News outlets reported on a non-existent horror character encouraging suicide, causing YouTube to purge innocent animation videos that were falsely flagged.

44. The code name for the project that became YouTube was "Tune In." It was scrapped because the domain name was too expensive to purchase.

45. YouTube has been accused of "digital gerrymandering." Its algorithm has been shown to recommend increasingly extreme political content to users, pushing them to the fringes for the sake of engagement.

46. The most viewed YouTube video ever is a children's song. "Baby Shark Dance" has over 14 billion views, highlighting the platform's unanticipated and massive dominance in children's entertainment.

🤵 **47.** The site's classic "star" rating system (1-5 stars) was a failure. Almost every video was rated either 1 or 5 stars, providing no useful data, which is why it was replaced with a simple like/dislike system.

💔 **48.** The platform has a secret "quality score" for every creator. This hidden score, based on audience retention and engagement, determines how widely their videos are promoted by the algorithm, often without their knowledge.

🧠 **49.** The first video to ever hit 1 million views was a Nike ad featuring Ronaldinho in 2005. It proved the platform's viral potential to major brands overnight.

⚖️ **50.** A single user's copyright claim can instantly demonetize a video. This system, designed to protect creators, is often weaponized by individuals and companies to censor critics or steal revenue through false claims.

TABLE OF CONTENTS

CHAPTER 1: THE EARLY INTERNET LANDSCAPE

- *The state of online video before YouTube*
- *Emerging technologies that set the stage*
- *Cultural and economic conditions favoring a new platform*

CHAPTER 2: THE FOUNDERS OF YOUTUBE

- *Backgrounds of Chad Hurley, Steve Chen, and Jawed Karim*
- *How they met at PayPal and formed their partnership*
- *Early funding and brand creation*

CHAPTER 3: THE LAUNCH OF YOUTUBE

- *Beta testing and initial user reactions*
- *First public releases of the platform*
- *Key features introduced at launch*

CHAPTER 4: GROWTH AND EARLY POPULARITY

- *Rapid user adoption and word-of-mouth marketing*
- *Iconic early videos and community engagement*
- *Technical strides to handle viral growth*

CHAPTER 5: KEY MILESTONES IN THE FIRST YEAR

- *Major site updates and improvements*
- *Influential partnerships and collaborations*
- *User-generated trends that shaped the platform*

CHAPTER 6: YOUTUBE'S RELATIONSHIP WITH GOOGLE

- *Google's initial interest in YouTube*
- *Acquisition discussions and agreement details*
- *Immediate impact on the platform's direction*

CHAPTER 7: COMMUNITY BUILDING & USER-GENERATED CONTENT

- *Tools and features that fostered user interaction*
- *The role of comments, ratings, and subscriber counts*
- *Growth of niche communities and fandoms*

CHAPTER 8: THE RISE OF VIRAL VIDEOS

- *Defining what "viral" meant in early YouTube culture*
- *Memorable videos and their global impact*
- *How virality influenced content creation practices*

CHAPTER 9: EARLY CHALLENGES AND COMPETITORS

- *Bandwidth costs and site maintenance hurdles*
- *Rival platforms vying for user attention*
- *YouTube's strategies to stand out in a crowded market*

CHAPTER 10: LEGAL BATTLES AND CONTROVERSIES

- *Copyright issues and takedown policies*
- *High-profile lawsuits and their outcomes*
- *User accountability and the future of open platforms*

CHAPTER 11: IMPACT ON CULTURE AND MEDIA

- *How YouTube changed entertainment consumption*
- *Influence on journalism, music, and independent creators*
- *Shifts in viewer expectations and distribution models*

CHAPTER 12: YOUTUBE'S ROLE IN THE 2008 U.S. ELECTIONS

- *Political campaigning on the platform*
- *Citizen journalism and user-generated debate highlights*
- *Regulatory discussions and free speech concerns*

CHAPTER 13: INTERNATIONAL EXPANSION

- *Local language sites and adapting to different markets*
- *Challenges in regions with limited internet infrastructure*
- *Growing influence on global internet culture*

CHAPTER 14: EVOLVING TECHNOLOGY AND FEATURES

- *Transition from Flash to new video standards*
- *Introduction of HD and user-friendly mobile apps*
- *Efforts to improve reliability and video quality*

CHAPTER 15: THE GROWTH OF PARTNERSHIPS AND MONETIZATION

- *Early ad integration and revenue-sharing initiatives*
- *Partnership programs that supported creators*
- *Balancing user experience with commercial interests*

CHAPTER 16: THE EMERGENCE OF YOUTUBE STARS

- *Rise of influencer culture and dedicated fan bases*
- *Monetizing content through sponsorships and collaborations*
- *YouTube's impact on shaping digital celebrities*

CHAPTER 17: THE EARLY INFLUENCE ON TRADITIONAL MEDIA

- *TV networks and film studios respond to user-driven content*
- *Crossovers between YouTube creators and mainstream outlets*
- *Shifting power dynamics in entertainment*

CHAPTER 18: CORPORATE CHANGES AND GROWING PAINS

- *Organizational restructuring and leadership shifts*
- *Challenges with policy enforcement and user discontent*
- *Adapting to rapid growth and increasing user demands*

CHAPTER 19: THE TRANSITION INTO MAINSTREAM ENTERTAINMENT

- *YouTube's infiltration into everyday life*
- *Partnerships with major brands and production companies*
- *Moving beyond user content and experimental programming*

CHAPTER 20: LEGACY OF THE EARLY YOUTUBE ERA

- *Reflecting on the platform's foundational impact*
- *Influence on subsequent social media and video platforms*
- *Enduring lessons from YouTube's pioneering years*

CHAPTER 1: THE EARLY INTERNET LANDSCAPE

1. Introduction to the Pre-YouTube World

In the early 2000s, the internet was still growing. Many people relied on dial-up connections, which were slow. Websites often had simple layouts and limited interactivity. Online video was not easy to find. Most users stayed with basic text and low-resolution images because video files were large and bandwidth was expensive. When people wanted to share videos, they had to email small clips or use file-sharing services that often required special software. This was not convenient, and it kept online video from truly expanding.

During this time, social media platforms were just beginning. MySpace, launched in 2003, allowed users to personalize profiles with music and pictures. Friendster had arrived a bit earlier but struggled to handle its fast growth. Facebook started in 2004, but it was limited to college students. None of these sites specialized in video hosting, even if they allowed small clips or animated elements. It was clear there was a gap in the market for a platform devoted entirely to user-generated videos.

High-speed internet connections, known as broadband, were beginning to appear more widely in homes. However, this adoption was slow. Still, in many places, dial-up was the norm. Websites that wanted to host videos found it difficult to serve large files to people with slow connections. Servers were costly, and streaming software was not very robust. Services like RealPlayer existed, but they had problems. Videos would buffer too long or lose quality. All of this created a landscape where sharing video online was not just a technical challenge but also a financial one.

2. Early Video-Sharing Solutions and Their Limitations

Before YouTube, if you wanted to share a video, you might have tried using personal web pages or forums. You would post a link to a file that needed to be downloaded. The person on the receiving end then had to download the entire file before watching it. If the file was large, this could take hours on a dial-up connection. Additionally, websites hosting these files faced significant server strain. If too many people tried to access the file at once, it could cause bandwidth issues or even crash the host site.

Many small startups tried to address this problem. Some used peer-to-peer networks like BitTorrent to distribute large files more efficiently. However, this required users to install special applications and understand how peer-to-peer sharing worked, which was not user-friendly for the average person. At the same time, technology like Flash video was improving. Flash allowed for easier in-browser playback, removing the need for special media players. But the ability to encode and serve Flash videos was still not widespread or cheap.

This meant that if you wanted to watch a video on a website, you might have to install a specific plugin, wait for buffering, and hope your connection was good enough to handle it. Internet speeds varied greatly from one region to another. Many people in rural areas or developing countries simply could not manage large media files. All these factors contributed to a significant untapped demand. People wanted to share funny or interesting clips with friends and family, but the existing tools made it challenging.

3. The Rise of Social Networking and User-Generated Content
Even though video-sharing was tough, other forms of user-generated content were on the rise. Blogging platforms such as Blogger and LiveJournal gave people ways to publish text quickly. Photo-sharing sites like Flickr let users upload and share photos with ease. These services showed that people enjoyed creating and sharing their own content. It also demonstrated that a website devoted to content sharing could build strong communities.

As more people gained access to higher internet speeds at schools, libraries, and workplaces, they found opportunities to upload larger files. Some small sites tried to bring video sharing into the social media mix by letting users attach video clips to profiles, but most of these efforts were limited due to technical hurdles. Early video upload sites often had strict size limits. They might only allow a few megabytes per file, forcing anyone uploading video to compress it heavily, losing much of the quality.

Despite these roadblocks, the internet community was pushing for more ways to express itself. People were becoming comfortable with the idea of being both consumers and creators of online content. This cultural shift set the stage for a specialized site to take advantage of the growing trend in user-generated material. When that site appeared, it would need easy-to-use tools, good streaming technology, and enough server capacity to handle traffic from millions of users.

4. Economic and Cultural Factors Leading to Demand
Around 2004 and 2005, the global economy was relatively stable. Investors were looking for the "next big thing" in tech following the dot-com crash of the late 1990s and early 2000s. Social media and broadband expansion offered a glimpse of new opportunities. People were exploring new ways to spend time online. Broadband internet plans were becoming cheaper. This gave rise to a cultural shift where internet users expected more engaging multimedia experiences.

Mobile technology was also on the rise, but early smartphones had limited video capabilities. Still, camera phones were starting to appear, and more people could record short video clips of everyday life. This shift to personal video creation fueled the idea that if there was a convenient place to share and watch these clips, it could become hugely popular. Traditional media outlets were not yet offering on-demand video content in a straightforward way, so user-generated platforms had a chance to flourish.

In addition, people were becoming more comfortable sharing personal moments online. The stigma of posting personal content was lessening as blogging and photo-sharing became widespread. This meant a video-sharing site would likely see a large influx of personal videos once it made uploading and viewing them easy. The cultural moment was ripe for a significant change in how video was consumed and shared.

5. Technology Enablers: Flash and Streaming Protocols
One key part of YouTube's success was the technology that allowed videos to be played quickly in a web browser. Macromedia Flash (later acquired by Adobe) was widely used for animations and simple web games. By the mid-2000s, Flash could handle video playback. This meant that the average user didn't need to install specialized plugins or codecs to watch a video. All they needed was the Flash Player plugin, which most browsers had by default.

Flash made it possible for a single video file to be compatible across many different computer setups. Users didn't have to worry about whether a video was in Windows Media format, QuickTime, or RealPlayer format. YouTube's adoption of Flash video streaming cut through this confusion. It was a major leap forward in user experience. When you combined an easy upload process with a straightforward viewing experience, you got a platform that could reach a wide audience quickly.

Server infrastructure was another essential factor. As the cost of hosting and serving data began to drop, it became more plausible for a startup to store and stream thousands of videos at scale. Content Delivery Networks (CDNs) began to appear, which allowed websites to distribute heavy traffic across multiple servers. While YouTube's earliest days relied on simpler approaches, the concept of CDNs indicated a direction the market was heading: large-scale video services could become feasible if managed well.

6. Shifts in Online Culture Pre-YouTube
The internet culture around 2004 and 2005 was curious about viral content. Email forwards of funny clips or short animations like the "Star Wars Kid" or "Numa Numa Dance" were common. People liked sharing quick laughs and surprising content, but it was often done in a clumsy way. You had to download a video file from a random server or open a peculiar email attachment. This method wasn't safe or consistent.

Forums and message boards existed for niche interests, and these communities were ready for a simpler way to embed or link to videos. Humor, music videos, and personal vlogs were some of the main categories of content people wanted to share, but the infrastructure just wasn't there. A user might see a friend's cool video but have no easy method to pass it along. Often, the best they could do was share a link to a file hosting service.

As a result, many iconic internet memes spread in an ad hoc fashion. There was no single platform to gather view counts, comments, or "likes." This lack of centralization meant it was hard for creators to track how well their videos were doing. Additionally, viewers didn't have a single destination to explore trending videos. This situation set the stage for a site that could bring everything under one roof. It was a perfect storm of cultural readiness and growing technological capability, waiting for a bold idea.

7. The Dot-Com Bust and the Rebirth of Online Startups
The early 2000s saw the collapse of many internet companies during the dot-com bust. But by 2005, venture capitalists and entrepreneurs were starting to invest in new ideas. Social media, blogging, and web-based applications showed promise. They fit into the "Web 2.0" movement, which focused on user interaction, content creation, and collaboration.

In this environment, a video-sharing platform that leveraged user-generated content could attract attention from investors seeking the next big hit. However, some investors were cautious. Bandwidth expenses for video streaming could become huge if a service took off. At the same time, the success of MySpace showed that a platform could grow rapidly if it addressed user needs and became a cultural phenomenon. The right idea could get significant funding even if it had high infrastructure costs, as long as it showed massive user engagement potential.

8. Early Attempts at Streaming Services
Before YouTube, there were some attempts to create streaming platforms, but many were focused on music or professional content. Websites that tried to offer full-length movies or TV shows online ran into legal and licensing issues. Others tried to make their own video players, but these often caused compatibility problems. Some sites tried to use embedded Windows Media Player, RealPlayer, or QuickTime windows, leading to frustration among users who did not have the correct version installed.

None of these efforts solved the universal problem of "I want to upload my own video easily and let anyone watch it without special software." The video hosting market was fragmented. You had to hope that whoever wanted to see your clip had the right tools. This complexity slowed down the acceptance of online video beyond tech-savvy circles. A mainstream solution simply did not exist yet.

9. The Stage is Set for Innovation
By late 2004, the pieces were in place for a new kind of website to emerge. Flash video was stable enough for broad use. Broadband internet was spreading. People were ready for a platform that made sharing videos just as simple as sharing photos. The limitations of email attachments and specialized software were becoming more frustrating as more creative content appeared. A site offering a quick upload process, immediate playback, and user-friendly navigation could capture the imagination of a wide audience.

In addition, blogging and the concept of online identity were becoming more normalized. People were starting to see the internet not just as a tool for research or basic communication, but as a space for self-expression. Videos would be a natural extension of this trend. All it would take was a handful of pioneering thinkers who recognized the possibilities and had the technical know-how to execute a user-friendly platform.

10. The Founders' Background before YouTube
While this chapter does not dive into the specific backgrounds of Chad Hurley, Steve Chen, and Jawed Karim (that is for Chapter 2), it's worth noting that Silicon Valley was full of talented engineers, designers, and entrepreneurs who had watched the failures and successes of the dot-com era. Many of them saw an opportunity in user-generated content. Some were working at PayPal and other tech companies where they gained experience in handling large-scale online services.

This swirl of skills, ideas, and ambition made it possible for a small team to come together with a new concept. The standard model for a tech startup was also maturing. Entrepreneurs knew how to pitch ideas to venture capitalists. They understood the importance of designing services that were simple yet appealing. The idea of a "minimum viable product" was also taking root, meaning you could launch a service with basic features, then iterate rapidly to improve it based on user feedback.

11. Summary of the Pre-YouTube Environment
By the end of 2004 and the beginning of 2005, the internet was ready for a big change in how videos were shared. People had broadband connections more often. Social media sites showed that user-generated content was popular. Flash video technology was advanced enough to make

playback smooth and hassle-free for most users. Investors were looking for the next wave of web startups, and cultural shifts were leaning toward personal expression.

This was the world into which YouTube would be born. It was a world that wanted an easy solution for sharing and watching videos, one that did not require technical mastery to use. All the conditions were right for a platform to come in and transform the online landscape. In the following chapters, we will see how YouTube emerged in this environment and how it leveraged these favorable conditions to become a major force in internet history.

12. Cultural Curiosity and the Appetite for Video
It's important to understand that the appetite for video was huge, but it was largely unmet. People found ways to share short clips of interesting things, whether it was a funny moment with friends, a clip from a TV show, or a personal creative project. But these methods were always cumbersome. The only sites that did host videos typically had strict rules, size limits, or complicated processes. Early adopters kept searching for something better. They wanted a centralized platform where they could discover new videos, share their own, and engage with a growing community.

As soon as the right platform showed up, it was likely to go viral itself. The internet was primed for a service that was approachable by anyone with a camera and a desire to share. This cultural curiosity, combined with easier tools, would make YouTube's early days a rapid success story, as we will uncover in the following chapters.

CHAPTER 2: THE FOUNDERS OF YOUTUBE

1. Introduction: Who Are Chad Hurley, Steve Chen, and Jawed Karim?
Chad Hurley, Steve Chen, and Jawed Karim are the three individuals credited with creating YouTube. They came from diverse backgrounds but shared a passion for technology and innovation. Their collaborative dynamic would be a key factor in the early direction and success of YouTube. In this chapter, we explore their personal histories before they started YouTube, describing how they met, what inspired them, and how they formed a team that would launch a revolutionary video-sharing platform.

2. Chad Hurley's Early Life and Interests
Chad Hurley was born in Reading, Pennsylvania, in 1977. As a child, he showed an interest in the arts and technology. He enjoyed drawing, design, and later became fascinated with computers and the web. In high school, he focused on graphic design, even winning competitions. This blend of creative and technical talents would prove crucial when it came to branding and designing YouTube's early interface.

Hurley attended Indiana University of Pennsylvania, where he studied art. After college, he moved into the tech sector, drawn by the startup culture of the early 2000s. His design skills, combined with a knack for understanding user experiences, made him well-suited for roles where technology needed a human-friendly interface. Eventually, Chad found himself at PayPal, working on the company's logo and user interface design. This is where he would meet his future co-founders, forging friendships that revolved around creativity, technology, and the desire to build something new.

3. Steve Chen's Background and Technical Skills
Steve Chen was born in Taiwan in 1978 and later moved to the United States. He pursued a degree in computer science, demonstrating a strong aptitude for software engineering and system architecture. Like many young talents with an interest in coding, Chen was drawn to Silicon Valley's vibrant tech scene. He looked for opportunities where he could develop products that would reach millions of people.

Eventually, he, too, landed at PayPal. PayPal was a magnet for top engineering and design talent at the time. The startup environment at PayPal encouraged employees to think outside the box and propose new solutions for online transactions. Chen's skill set centered on building and optimizing systems that could handle large amounts of data and user traffic. This expertise would prove essential for launching and maintaining YouTube's infrastructure, which needed to handle tons of video uploads and streaming demands.

4. Jawed Karim's Role and Influences
Jawed Karim was born in 1979 in East Germany to a Bangladeshi father and a German mother. His family later immigrated to the United States, where Karim studied computer science at the University of Illinois at Urbana-Champaign, a renowned school for engineering and technology. During his college years, he gained a strong foundation in software development.

Karim was also part of the PayPal team, though he had a different role compared to Hurley and Chen. He was known for his analytical approach and keen insight into the challenges faced by online payment systems. Karim was more reserved than his co-founders but provided the critical thinking that often sparked new ideas. His interest in user-generated content and the potential of digital media shaped how the three founders thought about an online video platform.

5. How They Met at PayPal

The fact that all three future YouTube founders worked at PayPal is not just a coincidence. PayPal's startup culture encouraged innovation, rewarded bold ideas, and brought together some of the most forward-thinking minds in technology. This environment allowed Hurley, Chen, and Karim to collaborate on projects and see firsthand how to scale a company. They also learned about online user interactions and building a product that would cater to a global audience. These lessons would become valuable when they left PayPal.

The so-called "PayPal Mafia," a nickname for the group of early PayPal employees, included other notable figures like Elon Musk, Peter Thiel, and Reid Hoffman (who founded LinkedIn). Many of these individuals went on to create or fund some of the most significant tech companies of the 2000s. Being part of this network meant the future YouTube founders had access to a community of experienced entrepreneurs and venture capitalists.

6. The Spark of the Idea

Several stories float around about what exactly led to the idea for YouTube. One popular anecdote is that Chen and Hurley wanted to share video clips from a dinner party but found it difficult to do so. Another story suggests that the founders saw how people struggled to share tsunami footage after the devastating 2004 Indian Ocean earthquake. Karim also mentioned not finding a place to watch Janet Jackson's controversial Super Bowl halftime incident in 2004.

Regardless of the precise event, the three recognized a simple truth: there was no central, easy-to-use website for sharing videos online. They saw that picture-sharing sites and social networks were growing fast, but video was still lagging. They believed a platform dedicated solely to video uploads and playback would fill a huge gap in the market.

7. Early Brainstorming Sessions

Once the idea began to take shape, the three co-founders held informal meetings to discuss what the site might look like. Chad Hurley thought about how to make the platform visually appealing and intuitive. Steve Chen focused on the technical aspects of how to store, transcode, and stream videos. Jawed Karim contributed ideas on user engagement, thinking about how comments, ratings, and a sense of community could form around shared videos.

During these brainstorming sessions, they decided to use Flash video to simplify playback. They also agreed that the service would allow anyone to upload videos without special knowledge. This meant building user-friendly tools for uploading, processing, and embedding videos. The founders also considered how to handle user accounts, privacy settings, and the ability to share or embed videos on other sites. Even in the early stages, they aimed for a platform that would encourage social interaction around video content.

8. Funding the Initial Launch
Starting a video-streaming site in 2005 wasn't cheap. Servers, bandwidth, and storage were expensive. The founders pooled together some personal funds, and they also got support from investors who saw the potential in a user-driven video platform. Their connections from PayPal helped open doors to venture capitalists who were willing to take a risk on a novel idea.

Sequoia Capital, for instance, played a big role in funding YouTube's early development. The funds covered office space, server equipment, and employee salaries. This financial backing gave the founders time and resources to refine the platform before launching it publicly. Their goal was to create a site that was reliable enough to handle real traffic from day one, minimizing the possibility of server crashes or painfully slow load times.

9. The YouTube Name and Brand
Chad Hurley's design background was pivotal in creating YouTube's name and logo. The concept behind "YouTube" was simple: "You" represent the user, and "Tube" was a slang term for television, suggesting a personal broadcast station. The name was catchy and easy to remember. The logo was similarly straightforward, featuring a red tube-like shape around the word "Tube." This simplicity played a role in building brand recognition. People could quickly recall and spell the name, which helped the site gain traction through word of mouth.

10. Early Teamwork Dynamics
Each founder had a specific role, but they also wore many hats in true startup fashion. Hurley might be working on the overall look of the website one day and coordinating with investors the next. Chen spent long hours setting up servers and coding the backend to ensure videos could be uploaded, converted, and played quickly. Karim focused on usability and new features to make the site appealing for early adopters. Their synergy came from a shared vision: a site where uploading and watching videos felt natural and straightforward.

They all understood the importance of feedback. They tested early versions of the site with friends, gathering opinions on what was confusing or frustrating. This feedback loop allowed them to make tweaks before going public. They knew that a poor first impression could hurt adoption, so they pushed hard to make each feature as smooth as possible.

11. Early Office Setup
YouTube's first office was small and modest. Some employees recall it being cramped with

computer monitors and servers. The environment was energetic. Conversations about technical issues overlapped with creative discussions about the site's look and feel. The founders wanted to keep a startup mentality, encouraging quick decision-making and welcoming bold ideas. They believed that speed was crucial if they wanted to capture the market before a competitor arrived with a similar idea.

Morale was generally high, despite the long hours and the uncertainty that comes with any startup. The team saw progress every day, with new features being implemented and tested. Early testers uploaded random home videos, short clips, and experimental content. The site was shaping up to be exactly what they had envisioned—a user-friendly hub for video sharing.

12. Vision for the Future

Even at this early stage, the founders discussed the broader impact they hoped YouTube would have. They dreamed of a day when people could broadcast themselves to the world without needing a major TV network. They saw how the platform could empower creative talent that otherwise might never be discovered. They also recognized the potential for educational content, allowing students and teachers to share lessons online.

However, they also knew there would be obstacles. Handling copyrighted material was one concern. They discussed how to discourage users from uploading material they did not own. The legal framework for online video was murky, with few precedents for how a platform should handle user-uploaded content. They realized they would need a system in place for takedown requests and for dealing with potential lawsuits.

13. Karim's Partial Departure

An interesting fact in YouTube's early history is that Jawed Karim stepped back from day-to-day operations while he went to pursue a master's degree in computer science at Stanford. He remained an adviser and held a stake in the company, but he was less involved than Hurley and Chen in the day-to-day management. This decision led to some differences in ownership shares later, but Karim's influence on YouTube's earliest concepts was still significant.

Karim's involvement during this period was more at a strategic level. He provided input on features and user engagement strategies. He also helped shape the approach to creating a community-driven site. While he was not in the office every day, his voice continued to inform key decisions.

14. Early Public Perception of the Founders

When YouTube started to gain attention, technology blogs and news outlets highlighted the founders' PayPal connection. They were perceived as part of a new wave of entrepreneurs who had practical experience in running large-scale online services. The press was intrigued by their claim that they could solve the video-sharing problem once and for all. Early write-ups typically praised the site's ease of use and smooth playback, crediting the technical expertise of Chen, Karim, and the design sense of Hurley.

The founders often came across as easygoing and open to experimentation. They did not present themselves as industry disruptors at first. Instead, they emphasized how they wanted to make video sharing less painful. This modest approach contrasted with some startups that proclaimed they would "change the world" from day one. In reality, YouTube would indeed change the online world, but the founders let the site's growth speak for itself.

15. The Role of Networking and Connections
Having worked at PayPal, the founders were familiar with several influential people in Silicon Valley. They used their connections to secure meetings and pitch sessions with venture capitalists. This network also helped them recruit early employees who understood large-scale data systems. While the name "PayPal Mafia" was sometimes used jokingly, it pointed to a real community of former PayPal employees who supported each other's ventures.

This network effect accelerated YouTube's momentum. Word spread quickly through investor circles that something special was brewing at YouTube. By the time the site was ready to go live, the founders had not only financial backing but also a network of supporters who championed the product at tech events and in online forums.

16. Foundational Values: Simplicity and Community
From the outset, the founders agreed that simplicity would be YouTube's hallmark. They wanted a design that even a casual internet user could navigate. Uploading a video should require no special knowledge of formats or encoding. The community aspect was also crucial. Users should be able to comment on videos, rate them, and share them easily. These features might seem obvious now, but in 2005 they were fresh ideas. Many existing sites were cluttered or demanded advanced technical knowledge.

The focus on community extended to user profiles, video tags, and recommended videos. The founders believed that people would keep coming back if they felt a sense of belonging or discovered interesting new content. This user-centric design approach was not just a method; it was a value system. They placed the user experience first, confident that a strong community would fuel the site's viral growth.

17. Lessons from PayPal Applied to YouTube
At PayPal, the founders had seen the power of viral adoption. Users recruited other users because the service was useful and solved a pressing problem—sending money online. YouTube had a similar potential for viral spread, but in the context of sharing fun or meaningful video clips. At PayPal, they also learned about the significance of trust and security. For YouTube, the equivalent challenges involved maintaining reliable uptime, fast video playback, and a clear policy on acceptable content.

Another lesson was that scale can be both an opportunity and a risk. When PayPal grew very fast, it attracted hackers, scammers, and spammers. YouTube's founders anticipated that if their site became large, they would need robust measures to moderate content and deal with malicious activities. The site was meant to be open to everyone, which was an asset but also a liability if people used it to distribute inappropriate or copyrighted materials.

18. Early Skepticism
Not everyone was convinced YouTube would succeed. Some critics pointed out the enormous bandwidth costs. Others questioned whether people really wanted to watch low-resolution videos filmed by amateurs. A few also noted that big players in media and technology could easily clone the service. The founders took these criticisms seriously but believed their head start, user-friendly approach, and brand identity would give them a strong competitive advantage.

They also felt that technology was moving in their favor. Broadband was spreading rapidly, and camera phones were becoming more common. Even though the first videos might be grainy or amateurish, they believed that better devices and faster connections would improve the overall quality of uploaded content. Over time, the site could host a broad range of videos, from personal diaries to short films, music videos, and anything else users wanted to create.

19. Final Preparations Before Launch

As the founders moved closer to launching YouTube, they spent countless hours testing. They made sure the uploading process worked smoothly and that the site could handle spikes in traffic. They also set up basic guidelines for community standards, though these were still evolving. Internally, they debated whether the site should enforce strict video length limits. They chose to allow fairly short videos at first, believing people would mostly share brief clips. This limit also helped them manage bandwidth costs in the early days.

They looked into ways to promote the site. Word of mouth and online communities were a starting point. They also considered direct outreach to content creators who might be interested in showcasing their work. The strategy was simple: if they got enough interesting videos on the platform, more viewers would come. As viewers increased, more people would be inspired to upload their own videos.

CHAPTER 3: THE LAUNCH OF YOUTUBE

1. Introduction and Setting the Stage

By early 2005, Chad Hurley, Steve Chen, and Jawed Karim were ready to turn their idea into a reality. They had secured initial funding, set up a small office, and decided on a clear mission: make video sharing easy for everyone. At that time, most people still relied on slow or moderately fast internet connections, but broadband was expanding. Many internet users wanted a centralized place to watch and share video clips without the hassle of downloading files or dealing with multiple media players.

The founders believed their platform would fill a gap in the online world. They realized that if they could deliver a streamlined way for people to upload, view, and share videos, the site might catch on quickly. Their brainstorming led them to focus on three main pillars: **simplicity**, **community**, and **openness**. These pillars would guide them as they prepared to launch YouTube in a beta form.

This chapter explores that delicate phase when YouTube moved from concept to public beta. We will see the hurdles the founders faced, how they encouraged early adoption, and why the first user reactions were so important to the website's future. It was a time of uncertainty and excitement—uncertainty because the founders did not know if they could handle technical demands and user interests at scale, and excitement because they believed they had a groundbreaking idea.

2. Domain Registration and Early Beta Plans

YouTube's official domain name registration date—February 14, 2005—has become a small piece of internet lore. Interestingly enough, "youtube.com" was not their first idea. Various domain names were discussed, but they eventually settled on something short, memorable, and reflective of the user-centric approach. "You" represented the individual uploading or watching, and "Tube" was a casual reference to television. The combined name hinted at a user's personal broadcast channel.

In early 2005, the founders spent much of their time setting up the core infrastructure for a beta release. They had to make sure the site was stable enough that early testers wouldn't be frustrated by slow loading times or constant errors. Bandwidth, file storage, and reliable video playback were top concerns. While they didn't expect millions of users right away, they wanted to be prepared for significant growth if word-of-mouth spread quickly.

They arranged a small "friends and family" beta test, inviting people they trusted to upload random home videos, short clips, or any content they had on hand. This phase was crucial. The founders needed real-world feedback from everyday internet users, not just tech-savvy testers. During these early trials, they discovered bugs in the video uploading process, encountered mismatched audio, and saw how important it was to handle different file formats. Because of these lessons, the site underwent constant tweaks before they opened it up to a wider audience.

3. Designing a User-Friendly Interface

From the beginning, Chad Hurley's background in design influenced YouTube's layout. He believed in clean, straightforward pages without flashy clutter. When users came to YouTube, they would see a simple homepage showcasing a handful of featured videos, a search bar, and clear links for uploading content. This layout was a sharp contrast to many other video or media sites at the time, which felt crowded with advertisements or complicated menus.

The first version of YouTube's interface included large "Upload" buttons and basic instructions on how to post a video. The founders wanted even a novice internet user to feel comfortable trying it out. Once a video was uploaded, the site handled the transcoding behind the scenes, converting it into a standardized format viewable in a Flash video player. This consistency across browsers and operating systems was a huge deal. No extra downloads or plugins were required beyond the commonplace Flash Player, which most people already had.

They also added a simple profile system. Users could create an account, upload videos, and see a list of their uploads in one spot. Others could click on the username to view the user's channel page—an early version that included only a few details like "username," "joined date," and a small area for personal info. Over time, these profile pages would evolve into more robust channels, but in early 2005, they were minimal by design.

4. "Me at the zoo"—YouTube's First Video

One of the earliest videos ever uploaded to YouTube was "Me at the zoo," posted by Jawed Karim on April 23, 2005. It is often cited as the first official YouTube video. Shot at the San Diego Zoo, the short clip features Karim standing in front of elephant enclosures, remarking about elephants' "really, really, really long trunks." As mundane as this clip may seem, it represented something revolutionary at the time: a normal person uploading a casual moment to a website where anyone in the world could watch it instantly.

"Me at the zoo" set the tone for the kind of personal, homegrown content YouTube could host. It was a departure from professional, polished videos. Instead, it showcased ordinary life, captured spontaneously on camera. This concept of authentic, personal videos would become one of YouTube's main attractions in its early days. Users realized they didn't need a production team or specialized equipment. A simple digital camera or phone could record everyday experiences worth sharing.

Karim's short video remains a symbol of YouTube's humble origins. It reminded viewers and potential uploaders that the site wasn't about high-budget projects or official broadcasts. Instead, it was about real people sharing real moments. The approachability of that first clip encouraged others to try uploading their own videos, even if those videos seemed unremarkable at first glance.

5. Encouraging Users to Upload

One big question the YouTube team faced was how to get people to post videos. They knew that if the site became a ghost town with very few uploads, viewers would lose interest and leave. To counter this, the founders decided to make uploading not just simple but also somewhat fun. They allowed basic tags, so users could categorize their clips under broad terms like "funny," "pets," or "music." Browsing by these tags gave watchers a way to discover new content.

They also introduced an "Upload Now" prompt in visible areas of the site. Any time a user visited, they could see opportunities to share something. While these prompts might seem obvious, they were pioneering at the time. Other websites buried their upload or share functions, assuming it was only for advanced users. YouTube turned it into a central activity. The message was clear: This site is for everyone, and your videos are welcome.

Early on, YouTube had no specific monetization or partnership program. Users posted videos mainly for fun or to show off personal moments to friends and family. Without that financial incentive, the company had to rely on the enjoyment factor. The more people found amusement or appreciation in watching and sharing clips, the more they'd be motivated to post new content. That cycle of uploading and viewing created a core community that helped YouTube expand.

6. Beta Testers, Word-of-Mouth, and User Feedback

After refining the site internally, the founders expanded the beta test to broader circles. They emailed colleagues, tech enthusiasts, and friends of friends, inviting them to try YouTube. Word-of-mouth began to spread through casual conversations and online forums. People started telling each other, "Check out this site where you can watch short videos right away—no need to download anything."

Beta testers provided valuable feedback. Some found the upload limits restrictive. Others commented that the video quality was too low. There were also questions about whether the site would always remain free. The founders took these notes seriously, adjusting file size limits, refining the compression quality, and making it clear that YouTube did not plan to charge viewers or uploaders.

Even though this was a time before social media platforms were as large as they are today, there were still popular message boards, email lists, and small online communities. YouTube quickly popped up in discussions about new websites worth exploring. Some internet users also wrote blog posts praising the simplicity of the upload and playback features. This organic publicity provided momentum without the founders having to spend a lot on advertising.

7. The Embed Feature and MySpace Synergy

One of YouTube's most impactful early innovations was the "embed" feature. It allowed users to copy a small snippet of code and paste it into their personal blogs or other websites. This meant videos could appear outside YouTube's domain, yet still be hosted by YouTube's servers. If someone embedded a video on their personal site, viewers there could watch it without leaving the page. This convenience was a game-changer and accelerated YouTube's spread across the internet.

Another crucial piece of synergy occurred with MySpace, a popular social networking site at the time. MySpace users loved customizing their profile pages, adding music, images, and personal flair. With YouTube's embed code, they could showcase videos directly on their MySpace pages. This let MySpace users share everything from birthday clips to short comedic sketches they found interesting. As MySpace boasted tens of millions of members, YouTube videos quickly reached a huge audience. It became common to see MySpace profiles featuring embedded YouTube content, effectively advertising YouTube to countless new viewers.

This embedding practice drove traffic back to YouTube itself. If someone discovered a fun video on a friend's MySpace page, they often clicked through to YouTube to explore more. As a result, YouTube's user base grew swiftly, fueled by the curiosity of social media users who wanted more interesting or amusing clips to watch. Embedding was not entirely new in concept, but YouTube executed it so smoothly that it felt revolutionary. It turned the platform into a central hub for internet videos.

8. The Five-Star Rating System and Early Comments

From the start, the founders understood that community involvement would keep people coming back. Simply letting people watch videos wasn't enough; they wanted viewers to feel engaged. To achieve this, YouTube introduced a five-star rating system. After watching a clip, users could rate it from one to five stars. This gave immediate feedback to the uploader and helped the site showcase top-rated content to others. It was a quick way to gauge popularity and sentiment.

The comment section was another key feature. Users could leave remarks, ask questions, or offer compliments directly under a video. This interaction made the viewing experience more social and less passive. Uploader and viewer could have a conversation, which often led to a sense of virtual camaraderie. Over time, heated debates, supportive messages, and in-jokes populated many comment sections, reflecting the diversity of opinions and personalities online.

Although moderating comments was not a heavy focus in the earliest days, the founders kept an eye on how discussions evolved. They were aware that as the platform grew, they might need stronger moderation tools. For the moment, though, they were more concerned with nurturing a lively community rather than imposing strict guidelines. The idea was to encourage as much user interaction as possible, trusting that constructive engagement would keep people hooked and generate fresh content.

9. Initial Press Coverage and First Recognitions

As the beta phase progressed, tech-savvy bloggers and smaller online news outlets began writing about YouTube. Headlines usually emphasized how easy the site was to use. Some articles drew attention to the possibility that YouTube could become the "Flickr of video" (Flickr being a successful photo-sharing platform at the time). A few early adopters hailed YouTube as the next evolution of social media, but the founders kept their goals modest publicly. They primarily highlighted user convenience.

In mid-2005, a handful of larger technology publications took notice. They wrote short pieces describing YouTube as an emerging player in the video-sharing space, though there were other startups also trying similar concepts. YouTube's advantage was its simple interface, Flash-based playback, and the growing library of user-uploaded content.

While there was no massive, mainstream media spotlight yet, these smaller waves of coverage helped validate YouTube's approach. Readers who clicked on the site after reading a blog post found an interface that worked, an interesting variety of videos, and an opportunity to join the community. This positive reception from niche tech circles hinted that YouTube might eventually capture a bigger audience if they continued to improve and scale.

CHAPTER 4: GROWTH AND EARLY POPULARITY

1. Introduction: Stepping into the Public Eye

By mid-2005, YouTube was no longer just a curiosity for beta testers and tech insiders. The wider internet community was beginning to discover it. Traffic was climbing, and more videos appeared on the site each day. As user numbers grew, so did the challenges. The founders had to figure out how to pay for expanding bandwidth needs, maintain the site's stability, and keep the experience user-friendly.

In this chapter, we look at how YouTube handled its first major growth wave. We'll examine the types of content that flourished, the community's reactions, and the creative ways the site managed to keep pace with user demand. We will also explore some of the earliest "viral" hits that put YouTube on the map, even if they weren't yet the massive global phenomena seen in later years. It was a dynamic time when the platform's potential was quickly becoming obvious to anyone paying attention.

2. Expanding Content Categories

Early YouTube uploads covered a wide spectrum. There were short vlogs (video blogs), personal diaries, funny skits, pet videos, and even the occasional tutorial. People tested the waters to see what kind of response they would get. Some posted clips of family gatherings or homemade music videos. Others showcased random, humorous events captured on camera. Because the site had no strict focus, it naturally became a melting pot for creativity.

In these early months, the founders noticed certain patterns. Comedy sketches often attracted attention, as did clips of pets doing amusing tricks. Personal vloggers found a small but loyal audience that engaged with them in the comments. The variety helped keep the site interesting. A visitor who came for cat videos might end up discovering a musician playing original songs in a bedroom recording, or a user ranting about a recent event in the news. This eclectic blend set YouTube apart from traditional media channels, which typically produced polished content around specific themes.

Though the site had a search feature and basic tags, it did not yet have advanced recommendation algorithms. Still, people stumbled upon new videos through related tags, user profiles, and the five-star rating system. Because of this, there was a sense of serendipity: you never knew exactly what you'd find next. For many, that was part of the fun.

3. Rapid Increase in User Accounts

During the summer of 2005, a notable surge in user registrations took place. Word-of-mouth was still a major driver, and embedding continued to be a vital source of traffic. Each time someone placed a video player on a blog or MySpace page, more viewers were introduced to YouTube. Curious viewers often created their own accounts to comment, rate videos, or upload something of their own.

With this growth, the founders tracked metrics like unique visitors, page views, and uploads per day. They noticed that many users returned multiple times per week—an early sign of strong user engagement. Once people discovered videos they liked, they came back to see if there were updates or fresh content from the same uploader. Friendships and small fan bases began to form around popular vloggers or comedic channels, although the site's "channel" concept was still in its early iteration.

The spike in user accounts also meant more data to manage. Information about each user, their uploads, and their interactions had to be stored reliably. Steve Chen and the technical team raced to scale up the servers, optimizing code to handle increased load. They had to ensure videos would remain playable at all times, minimizing the dreaded "this video is not available" message.

4. Traffic Spikes and Technical Challenges

As YouTube's popularity took off, the company found itself dealing with technical challenges that could make or break a young startup. Video hosting was expensive because large files needed to be uploaded, stored, and streamed. Each new user might bring multiple video uploads, each requiring a significant amount of disk space. Then there was the bandwidth issue: playing those videos for thousands or millions of users required robust connections and more servers.

When a certain video went viral within a small community—perhaps a local band's music clip or a comedic sketch—it could cause traffic spikes. While this meant increased visibility for YouTube, it also tested the site's infrastructure. If too many people accessed the same video simultaneously, the site could slow down or crash. During these months, Steve Chen and other engineers often worked around the clock, monitoring server performance and rolling out fixes in real time.

Chad Hurley's design priorities had to align with technical realities. Adding too many features or heavy design elements could slow the site. The founders agreed that the user experience had to remain smooth even as they added features. This balancing act—between functionality, aesthetics, and raw technical capacity—became a day-to-day challenge.

5. Short Comedic Videos and Early Humor Trends

Though YouTube welcomed all sorts of content, short comedic videos emerged as a favorite among viewers in mid to late 2005. Uploaders discovered they could film quick sketches or parodies with a simple camcorder, then share them instantly. These videos often featured slapstick humor, silly voices, or everyday mishaps. Because the platform was new, people weren't overly concerned with production quality. They were more interested in originality and fun.

Early comedic hits often had a homemade charm. Sometimes, a friend group would reenact movie scenes or produce exaggerated "news broadcasts" about trivial events. Viewers enjoyed the authenticity, and the comment sections lit up with inside jokes. Even though these videos might have been rough around the edges, that rawness was part of the appeal—there was no barrier to entry, no polished script required.

Some creators experimented with character-based comedy, where the same persona appeared in multiple uploads. They might rant about daily life or perform comedic monologues in their bedrooms. This allowed them to develop a personal connection with their small audiences, who came back for more episodes. The comedic category quickly grew, foreshadowing a future where comedy channels and entertainers would have millions of followers on YouTube.

6. Small Collaborations and Community Building

One important aspect of YouTube's growth was the collaboration that happened among uploaders. Even in 2005, some creators realized they could cross-promote by featuring each other in videos or linking to one another's channels. This early sense of community helped retain users because they felt part of a social network, not just a random website to dump videos on.

Viewers, too, began to notice the same faces popping up. They enjoyed crossovers where two comedic personalities would appear together in a silly skit. These small-scale collaborations were often informal. There were no contracts or financial deals in place. People simply connected through the site's messaging system or comments and decided to create something jointly. This spirit of teamwork built a sense of belonging, as if everyone on YouTube was part of one big neighborhood experimenting with video.

Moderation was still minimal, which had its pros and cons. On the positive side, the limited policing allowed creativity to flow, and users generally felt free to upload what they liked. On the downside, mild trolling and rude behavior appeared in comments. The founders had to consider guidelines for the future, but in these early days, the overwhelming sentiment was excitement about new content rather than worry about hostility.

7. Brand Curiosity and Early Advertiser Interest

While YouTube did not yet have an established advertising system in 2005, some small companies and brands noticed the platform's growing user base. A few tried uploading promotional clips or commercials they had made for television. They hoped to reach a new, younger online audience. Although these efforts were modest, they hinted at a future where companies might see YouTube as a powerful marketing tool.

At this stage, the YouTube team did not invest heavily in courting advertisers. They were more focused on scaling the site and building a strong community. Still, the founders were aware that they would need a revenue model eventually. Venture capital funding could sustain them for a while, but not indefinitely. They quietly observed which videos drew the most views and thought about how targeted advertising could potentially align with those interests later on.

Brands that uploaded promotional content sometimes received positive feedback from users who found the ads entertaining or well-produced. In some cases, viewers discovered new products or music releases simply by stumbling upon an uploaded clip. This was a small taste of the platform's potential for viral marketing. Even though it was not a formal revenue stream at the time, it planted ideas that would shape YouTube's future approach to monetization.

8. Engaging the Early Community: Contests and Spotlights

Another way YouTube cultivated user interest was by featuring certain videos or channels on the front page. These "Featured Videos" or "Spotlights" could draw large amounts of traffic to a previously unknown creator. Sometimes, the founders or early staff members handpicked these videos based on humor, creativity, or social relevance. Later, they introduced simple automatic processes to cycle through popular or highly rated videos.

Occasionally, YouTube ran small contests or themed events to spur content creation. For example, they might announce a "Funny Pet Video Contest," encouraging users to upload clips of their pets doing amusing things. Winners would get showcased on the homepage, resulting in thousands of views. Though the prizes were usually just recognition, a front-page spotlight could significantly boost a user's subscriber count in those days.

These contests and spotlights served two purposes. First, they kept the community engaged, giving people a reason to keep creating. Second, they helped the site maintain a steady stream of fresh content. By highlighting diverse types of videos, YouTube ensured that new visitors saw a variety of clips right away, reflecting the platform's open-ended nature.

CHAPTER 5: KEY MILESTONES IN THE FIRST YEAR

---

1. Introduction: Why Milestones Matter

By the latter half of 2005, YouTube was beginning to show its potential as a leading online platform for sharing videos. Although the site was still young, several important milestones had already shaped its reputation and user base. These milestones were not always planned in a formal roadmap. Instead, they emerged as the team responded to user feedback, competition, and the general excitement surrounding online media at the time.

In this chapter, we explore the key events that made YouTube stand out during its first year. We look at how the website evolved to address user needs, handled sudden surges in traffic, and attracted attention from both the media and other tech companies. These moments helped YouTube transform from a promising startup into a recognized name among internet users. Understanding these milestones paints a clearer picture of YouTube's quick rise and how it laid the groundwork for future growth.

2. Moving Beyond Beta: Official Launch

2.1. Transitioning Out of Beta Testing

After several months of beta testing in early to mid-2005, the team felt confident that YouTube could handle a broader audience. The beta phase had allowed them to fix bugs, fine-tune the uploading process, and gather user reactions about the platform's layout. During this time, the founders and the small YouTube staff worked nearly nonstop to ensure the site's core features were stable. Their main concerns included:

- **Server reliability**: They needed enough server capacity to handle more uploads and simultaneous viewers.
- **Encoding efficiency**: Videos had to be processed quickly to keep users happy.
- **User interface clarity**: New visitors had to instantly understand how to find videos or upload their own.

By mid- to late 2005, the team decided the site was ready for a more official debut. Although the term "official launch" might sound like a grand event, in reality, it was more of a rolling process.

The team simply removed many of the "beta" labels from the site and began referring to YouTube as a fully operational web service.

2.2. Early Launch Buzz

As YouTube shifted from beta to live status, a wave of internet chatter helped spread the word. Tech blogs wrote short pieces about this video-sharing platform that had graduated from its test phase. Some mainstream news outlets also noted how YouTube was part of a growing trend of "Web 2.0" services, a term then used to describe interactive, user-driven websites. Though YouTube did not hold a flashy launch party or major press conference, the buzz generated by enthusiastic users served as effective publicity.

The official launch also coincided with a jump in daily visitors. More people arrived each day, curious to see what YouTube offered. In a sense, YouTube had reached its first major milestone simply by proving that it could move out of beta testing and continue operating smoothly as the number of users kept climbing.

3. Growing Recognition in Tech Circles

3.1. Early Awards and Accolades

Not long after its official launch, YouTube began to receive nods from various tech publications. Some magazines recognized it in "Best of the Web" or "Top Emerging Sites" lists, praising the site's simplicity and the potential it held for user-generated video. While these early awards were often small-scale, they validated the founders' efforts to make an approachable video-sharing service.

Word spread within Silicon Valley investment circles as well. Venture capitalists who had initially taken a cautious approach toward video platforms started to see YouTube as a leader in its field. A common sentiment among investors was that although video-sharing was expensive in terms of bandwidth, YouTube seemed to be the site best positioned to capture the mainstream audience that was quickly adapting to high-speed internet.

3.2. Public Appearances at Conferences

Chad Hurley, Steve Chen, and Jawed Karim also occasionally appeared at tech meetups or small conferences, sharing the story behind YouTube's creation. These presentations were usually informal. They did not present themselves as revolutionary pioneers. Instead, they spoke about how they tried to solve everyday problems related to video distribution. Yet, attendees recognized that YouTube might be more than just another startup; it was rapidly becoming a hub for online entertainment, news clips, and personal expression.

These conference appearances helped the founders connect with potential business partners and other innovators in the tech space. Although no major collaborations sprang up immediately, seeds were planted for future partnerships that would help the site grow. The positive reception at these events was another sign that YouTube's brand was steadily gaining momentum.

4. Development of the Featured and Categories Pages

4.1. Showcasing User Content

One of the unique aspects of YouTube during its first year was how it highlighted user-created videos on the homepage. Rather than focusing on professional productions, the founders believed that everyday people uploading personal clips deserved exposure. They created a "Featured Videos" section that would rotate through selected content. This provided regular visitors with a quick way to discover interesting or entertaining videos.

As more categories of content emerged—such as comedy, music, pets, sports highlights, and personal vlogs—the site added simple category tabs. These tabs helped users browse videos aligned with their interests. For instance, someone primarily interested in comedic sketches could click on "Comedy" to see top-rated or recently uploaded videos in that genre.

4.2. Encouraging Diverse Participation

These new features helped shape a culture where both established creators and newcomers had a chance to shine. If a user uploaded a video that caught the attention of YouTube staff, it could end up on the Featured page, leading to a sudden influx of views and comments. This possibility drew more and more people to upload their own content, hoping for a shot at this front-page spotlight.

By late 2005, the "Featured Videos" area had become a coveted spot. Creators would share tips on increasing their chances of being featured, such as using catchy thumbnails, writing interesting titles, or simply creating unique content. This user-driven environment meant that YouTube's library of videos kept expanding at an accelerating rate.

5. Handling Copyright Complaints and Early Content Policies

5.1. The Emergence of Copyright Issues

Early in YouTube's life, most uploads were personal videos or short clips of original content. However, it didn't take long for users to start posting copyrighted materials, such as music videos, television show segments, or movie snippets. This created legal concerns for the founders. They recognized that if YouTube became a haven for pirated media, they could face lawsuits that might threaten the site's survival.

At first, the company's approach to copyright issues was reactive. If a rightsholder complained about a video, YouTube would remove it. The site's Terms of Service stated that users should not upload content they did not own. However, enforcement was tricky. With the site growing quickly, it was impossible to check each upload manually.

5.2. Developing Takedown Procedures

To address these concerns, YouTube formalized a complaint and takedown process. Rightsholders could fill out a form, providing proof of ownership and a link to the infringing video. The video would then be removed, typically within a short timeframe. The team also explored automated tools to detect copyrighted material, but these systems were primitive compared to later solutions.

Despite these early efforts, YouTube encountered criticism from some media companies. They argued that YouTube was not doing enough to prevent unauthorized uploads. Others saw YouTube as a potentially valuable promotional channel if managed responsibly. This tension between open user uploads and legal compliance became a defining challenge for YouTube. While it was still early in the platform's life, these copyright debates signaled that more formal negotiations and solutions would be necessary in the future.

6. International Curiosity and the Start of Global Reach

6.1. Growing Interest Outside the United States

Even though YouTube was an American startup, it attracted attention from users around the world. Many non-English-speaking visitors found the site by stumbling upon embedded videos or hearing about it on internet forums. They watched clips and even uploaded some of their own, despite the interface still being in English. This was a sign that YouTube could have global appeal if it found ways to accommodate various languages and regional tastes.

Around late 2005, user statistics showed steady growth in countries outside the United States, including the United Kingdom, Canada, Australia, and parts of Europe and Asia. While the user interfaces were not localized yet, the simple design and universal appeal of video content helped YouTube gain traction. People uploading funny or interesting clips didn't always need subtitles, as many comedic or daily-life videos could be understood visually, regardless of language barriers.

6.2. Early Thoughts on Localization

The founders noticed these international visitors and began formulating ideas for local versions of the site. However, localizing YouTube would be no small task. They needed staff who could handle translation, community guidelines for different cultures, and potential legal differences related to content. In the first year, these localization plans remained in the brainstorming stage. The team was still small, and most energy went into scaling servers and keeping the main site running smoothly.

Even so, the presence of international users gave YouTube an early taste of what it would mean to be a global brand. It also highlighted how online video could unite people across borders, allowing them to share slices of everyday life. This was another milestone: YouTube was no longer seen only as a local or niche service. It was quickly becoming a place where the world could gather and watch.

7. Funding Boosts and Business Confidence

7.1. Additional Venture Capital

In 2005, after the site showed strong growth in traffic and uploads, YouTube secured more funding from venture capital firms such as Sequoia Capital. Early investors who had supported the platform recognized that YouTube's traction with users hinted at big things ahead. This fresh injection of capital allowed the company to hire more engineers, lease more servers, and explore broader marketing efforts.

Though the exact amounts were not always publicly detailed at the time, industry insiders speculated that YouTube was receiving several million dollars in each funding round. This was crucial because video hosting was among the most expensive services on the internet. Unlike a text-based platform, YouTube had to handle bandwidth-heavy video streams. Without investor support, the young company might have stalled or had to impose strict limits on users' uploads.

7.2. Hiring Key Talent

These new funds also let YouTube expand its workforce. The founders looked for experienced developers who could help with large-scale data management and streaming optimization. They also needed people to assist with customer support, user moderation, and communications. Bringing on more staff meant they could divide tasks more efficiently and continue pushing the product forward.

The ability to hire specialized talent was a major milestone because it moved YouTube from a small startup to a slightly larger operation. Although still far from being a big corporation, the team had more resources to handle the fast-growing user community. This laid the groundwork for future improvements, such as advanced search features, better video encoding, and eventually, more robust moderation tools.

8. Emerging Partnerships and Early Collaborations

8.1. Friendly Links with Media Outlets

Despite some tension around copyright, a few media companies saw YouTube's popularity as an opportunity. Smaller independent music labels or video producers discovered they could upload clips and drive fans to watch them on YouTube. If a video became popular, it served as free advertising. Some producers included watermarks or end cards directing viewers to their official websites or asking them to buy a product.

At this stage, these partnerships were informal. There were no major revenue-sharing deals or detailed contracts, but it was a hint that traditional media was not entirely hostile. Some understood that YouTube could act as a springboard for increasing brand awareness. In turn, YouTube welcomed any content that drew legitimate viewership, as it further boosted the platform's traffic and credibility.

8.2. Approaches from Other Startups

Smaller tech startups began to approach YouTube about integrating services or adding links between platforms. For example, some sites specialized in photo sharing or blogging and wanted to include YouTube video embeds as part of their user offerings. These cross-platform collaborations often benefited both sides by creating a seamless user experience.

These developments indicated that YouTube was becoming a recognized player in the broader ecosystem of web-based services. It showed that the platform was not merely a standalone site but part of a larger shift toward interactive online experiences. This evolution was a milestone in establishing YouTube as a central hub in the rapidly expanding social media landscape.

9. The Rise of Memorable Early Videos

9.1. Popular Clips and Their Impact

During YouTube's first year, certain videos gained remarkable popularity for that era. They might not have reached the millions of views we expect from viral hits today, but tens or hundreds of thousands of views were significant back then. Examples include humorous skits with friends, bizarre stunts, or low-quality music covers performed in living rooms. Viewers often shared these videos by emailing links to one another or embedding them on personal blogs.

Such videos drew repeated visits, as people would come back to show friends or see if the uploader had posted anything new. This behavior was different from traditional TV viewing, where content was scheduled and controlled by networks. On YouTube, users could watch favorite videos on demand, replay them, and discuss them in the comments. It was a milestone in how viewers interacted with media.

9.2. Early "Series" Formats

Even in its first year, a few dedicated creators tried producing episodic series. They would release new videos on a regular schedule, often featuring the same characters or themes. This was a new concept, as most early internet videos were one-offs. But these mini-shows, often homemade and very rough around the edges, gave viewers a reason to subscribe to a channel (though the "Subscribe" function was still basic) or bookmark the uploader's page.

Such early series, whether comedic or documentary-style, paved the way for the broader phenomenon of "web shows" that would later become popular on YouTube. The site's flexibility meant that anyone with a camera and an idea could produce a series, without needing a TV network's approval. Although these pioneering attempts did not all become mainstream hits, they signaled a shift toward continuous, creator-driven content.

CHAPTER 6: YOUTUBE'S RELATIONSHIP WITH GOOGLE

1. Introduction: A New Chapter for YouTube

By the end of 2005, YouTube's growing user base and the increasing volume of uploaded videos had made it a topic of conversation in Silicon Valley. Google, already an established tech titan, was closely monitoring trends in online media. While Google had its own video service (known simply as Google Video at the time), it was not achieving the same level of grassroots popularity that YouTube enjoyed. Users and critics often noted that YouTube was more user-friendly, more community-driven, and had more interesting, personal content.

This chapter examines how Google's interest in YouTube started to build, how early interactions between the two companies took shape, and why this relationship became one of the most significant milestones in YouTube's early history. The discussions and eventual negotiations with Google marked a shift from YouTube being a scrappy startup to becoming part of a major internet ecosystem.

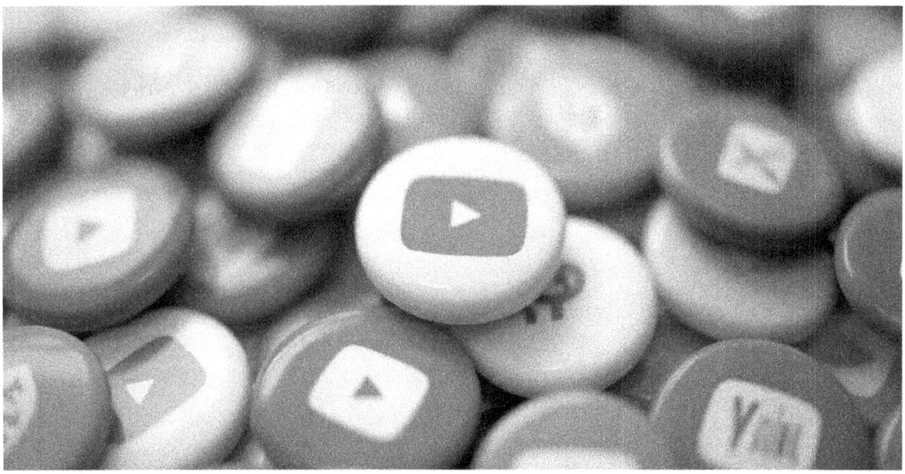

2. Google's Background in Video

2.1. The Launch of Google Video

Before YouTube entered the scene, Google had explored the idea of an online video service. Google Video launched in early 2005, not long before YouTube began to gain traction. However,

Google Video's initial approach was different. It aimed to provide a more curated experience, including professional content from media partners as well as a video search function across the internet. Uploading user-generated clips to Google Video was possible, but not the main focus.

Unlike YouTube's straightforward upload and watch system, Google Video's interface felt more complicated. Users needed to install special software to upload large files, and the processing time was often lengthy. There was also less emphasis on social interaction—commenting, rating, and community engagement were not as front-and-center as on YouTube.

2.2. The Challenges Google Faced in Video Sharing

Google was (and still is) an enormous company with many competing products. At that time, it was best known for its web search engine, email service (Gmail), and a few other tools. Video hosting presented unique challenges: huge storage requirements, high bandwidth costs, and potential legal risks. Even for a giant like Google, the question was whether hosting user videos was worth the trouble.

As Google observed YouTube's success, they faced a dilemma: Should they invest more heavily in improving Google Video, or consider partnering with—or even acquiring—a smaller company that already excelled at user-generated video? By late 2005, the popularity gap between Google Video and YouTube was widening, sparking serious conversations within Google about how to remain competitive in the online video market.

3. Early Contacts and Observations

3.1. Google's Quiet Monitoring

Silicon Valley is a tight-knit community in many ways. News of a fast-growing startup usually spreads quickly among venture capitalists, engineers, and executives. By mid-2005, Google staff were already using YouTube to watch and share casual video clips. Some Google employees remarked that YouTube's interface felt more fun and inviting than Google Video.

While no formal offers were made in these early days, there were occasional emails and casual chats between YouTube's founders and Google representatives at tech events. Google was known to keep tabs on rising platforms, sometimes forming informal relationships before making any serious proposals. From Google's perspective, YouTube was both an inspiration and a potential competitor.

3.2. The Founders' View of Google

Chad Hurley, Steve Chen, and Jawed Karim were well aware of Google's stature. They recognized that any positive connection with Google might bring more visibility to YouTube. However, they were also cautious. They had seen how large corporations could overshadow or absorb smaller startups, changing their culture and direction. At that point, YouTube's founders were focused on growing independently, securing funding, and maintaining creative control.

Even so, the idea of collaborating with Google was appealing, especially because YouTube's bandwidth costs were enormous. Google's infrastructure might offer solutions. The founders kept an open mind, not closing the door on any potential alliances that could help them scale.

4. Comparing User Experiences: YouTube vs. Google Video

4.1. Ease of Uploading and Viewing

One major reason for YouTube's edge over Google Video was how simple it was to upload clips. YouTube required only a few clicks to get a video online, and it automatically converted the file into Flash format. Google Video, on the other hand, asked users to download software or follow a more elaborate set of steps. This difference in user experience was a topic of discussion among Google staff, who realized they were behind in terms of simplicity.

For viewers, YouTube's community features—like easy sharing, embedding, commenting, and rating—also made the site more engaging. Google Video had some of these elements, but they were less prominent. People often described YouTube as a "fun place to hang out," while Google Video felt more utilitarian and search-oriented.

4.2. Content Breadth and Community Spirit

Another notable difference was the sheer variety of YouTube's user-generated content. Google Video tried to position itself as a platform for higher-quality or official videos, including TV show episodes and news clips, though its library was not very large. Meanwhile, YouTube was amassing countless amateur clips, music covers, comedic sketches, and personal vlogs. This gave YouTube a lively, unpredictable character that drew curious visitors who never knew what they might find.

The spirited discussions under YouTube videos also contributed to a sense of community. Although not always polite or well-moderated, the comment sections gave users a feeling that they were part of something interactive. Google Video did not inspire the same level of viewer engagement, reinforcing the idea that YouTube was more "alive" and people-centered.

5. Google Considers Acquisition Possibilities

5.1. Bandwidth and Infrastructure Challenges

Throughout 2005, YouTube's user base grew, and so did its operational expenses. Each day, more videos were uploaded, and the total watch time soared. Some early estimates suggested that YouTube was streaming millions of clips per day, which required a massive amount of bandwidth. Even with venture capital backing, the costs were daunting for a relatively small startup.

Google had the servers, data centers, and engineering expertise to handle large-scale bandwidth demands. If YouTube joined forces with Google, the smaller site would benefit from almost limitless infrastructure. From Google's standpoint, merging with YouTube could instantly place them in a leading position in the user-generated video arena, leapfrogging the uphill battle of improving Google Video from scratch.

5.2. Initial Internal Debates at Google

Inside Google, not everyone agreed on whether acquiring YouTube was the right strategy. Some executives were confident Google's own service could evolve. Others argued that YouTube's popularity was too big a lead to overcome and that an acquisition might be more efficient. The cost of any potential acquisition was also a factor: YouTube's value was rising alongside its user numbers. If Google waited too long, YouTube might become even more expensive—or get snapped up by a different tech giant.

By late 2005, the topic of acquiring YouTube had started to appear in some internal Google discussions. However, no formal negotiations began right away. Each side was still feeling out the possibilities, and YouTube's founders were not actively looking to sell. They were open to conversation but also keen to keep building their platform independently unless an outstanding offer came along.

6. The Role of YouTube's Rapid Growth in Negotiations

6.1. Traffic Metrics and Market Dominance

As 2005 turned into 2006, YouTube's statistics became more impressive. Reports indicated that the site was delivering several million video streams per day. Users were spending increasing amounts of time browsing from one clip to another. By spring of 2006, YouTube was being mentioned in mainstream media stories about the rise of online video, catapulting it further into the spotlight.

These numbers caught Google's attention even more. It became clear that YouTube was not just a fad. It was quickly becoming the default place for people to share personal clips or watch entertaining user content. If a giant like Google wanted to secure a major foothold in online video, striking a deal with YouTube began to look increasingly appealing.

6.2. Press and Public Speculation

Some media outlets speculated that YouTube could be the next big acquisition target in Silicon Valley. As a result, journalists asked YouTube's founders about their future plans, whether they would remain independent or seek a bigger partner. The founders usually responded by saying they were focused on growth and user satisfaction, sidestepping direct comments on any acquisition rumors.

Inside the company, employees sensed that something big might be on the horizon. They noticed more contacts with other major tech firms and realized that YouTube's exceptional growth was a bargaining chip in any negotiation. This environment contributed to a sense of excitement and uncertainty, as staff contemplated what a corporate partnership or acquisition would mean for the site's identity and mission.

7. Early Cooperation Efforts

7.1. Video Search Integration

Before any talk of acquisition became serious, Google and YouTube tested smaller forms of collaboration. One example involved improving video search. Google's powerful search engine could theoretically index YouTube's vast catalog of user-generated content, making it easier for users to find specific clips. While these efforts remained informal, they showed that Google recognized YouTube's growing library as a valuable database for search results.

7.2. Advertising and Revenue Discussions

Another area of informal cooperation revolved around potential advertising models. Google was a leader in online ads, thanks to programs like AdWords and AdSense. YouTube, on the other hand, had millions of eyeballs but no fully developed revenue strategy. There were occasional banner ads on the site, but no robust system for monetizing individual videos. Google employees hinted that if the two companies collaborated, they could leverage Google's advertising network to help YouTube—and its creators—earn money.

Though these talks were exploratory, they pointed to a broader strategic alignment: YouTube needed the infrastructure and ad technology that Google possessed, while Google saw YouTube's vibrant community as an ideal host for video ads or other promotional opportunities. This mutual benefit set the stage for more serious discussions about a formal partnership.

8. Obstacles and Concerns Around a Potential Deal

8.1. Fear of Losing Independence

From YouTube's perspective, the biggest worry was losing the unique culture and freedom that had made the site so successful. If YouTube became part of a giant corporation, would it still be able to move quickly, experiment, and focus on user-generated content without interference? The founders had built a community-centric platform, and they feared that too much corporate oversight might stifle the site's growth.

They also wondered how user trust might shift if YouTube were absorbed into a large company. Some users appreciated YouTube's scrappy startup vibe and might not welcome a corporate takeover. Maintaining that sense of authenticity and approachability was key for user loyalty.

8.2. Regulatory and Legal Considerations

On the other side, Google's lawyers raised concerns about the legal challenges YouTube faced, particularly around copyright violations. If Google bought YouTube, it would inherit these risks. Some at Google worried that the combined company might attract more scrutiny from media conglomerates, leading to expensive lawsuits.

Additionally, any deal of that size could draw the interest of regulators who might worry about monopolistic practices in the online video space. Although the market was still new and evolving, large acquisitions sometimes triggered official reviews. Both sides had to consider these legal angles before signing any agreements.

9. Tipping Points Toward Serious Negotiation

9.1. YouTube's Ongoing Bandwidth Strain

As 2006 progressed, YouTube's bandwidth bills continued to skyrocket. While ongoing funding rounds helped, there was always the chance that the platform's costs could outpace what investors were willing to supply. The founders realized that to keep up with user growth, they either needed an endless supply of venture capital or a partnership with a larger entity.

This need for financial stability and technical infrastructure was becoming a critical factor. Though YouTube could continue raising money in the short term, it might face diminishing returns if the site's expenses kept doubling every few months. A partnership with Google could solve these issues almost overnight, giving YouTube the freedom to focus on content and community.

9.2. Growing Sense of Urgency at Google

Simultaneously, Google executives felt urgency about capturing the online video market. While Google Video was still active, it lagged far behind YouTube. If Google waited too long, another tech giant (like Yahoo or Microsoft) could try to scoop up YouTube. Such a move would put Google at a disadvantage in a fast-growing sector.

These converging pressures—YouTube's massive costs and Google's desire to dominate online video—brought both sides closer to the idea of an acquisition. By mid-2006, discreet negotiations started to take shape, with lawyers, bankers, and senior executives discussing potential deal structures and valuations.

CHAPTER 7: COMMUNITY BUILDING AND USER-GENERATED CONTENT

1. Introduction: The Heart of Early YouTube

When YouTube began in 2005, it was not just a video-hosting site; it was a space for everyday people to upload clips and interact with one another. This set YouTube apart from traditional media platforms that only allowed passive viewing. On YouTube, people could **comment**, **rate**, and even **collaborate**, which helped form a sense of community around user-generated content. By late 2005 and into 2006, YouTube's user base started to realize that the platform was about more than just funny videos or random clips—it was a place where individuals could form bonds, share interests, and express themselves without major restrictions.

In this chapter, we explore how YouTube's earliest features—comments, channel pages, social interactions, and community guidelines—shaped the sense of belonging that developed among its users. We'll see how small groups formed, how early creators built followings, and how YouTube's growing culture influenced the entire concept of "online community" during a time when social media was still fairly new. This era laid the foundation for many of the community-driven elements that remain key to YouTube's identity.

2. The Root of Community: Comments and Ratings

A major difference between watching a video on YouTube and watching a video on a television screen was the ability for the audience to **respond immediately**. When users finished watching a clip, they could scroll down and type their thoughts, ask questions, or even criticize the uploader. This interaction might seem common now, but in 2005 and 2006, it was a novel approach to viewing media.

1. **Immediate Feedback Loop**
    - If someone posted a short comedy sketch, viewers could rate the video using YouTube's **five-star rating system** (for example, three stars for "okay," five stars for "loved it"). They could then leave a comment telling the creator what they liked or disliked. The uploader often replied in the same comment thread. This **immediate feedback** was highly motivational for creators, who suddenly saw that people worldwide could appreciate or critique their work in real time.
2. **Sense of Participation**
    - Unlike traditional TV or film, where production teams had to guess audience reactions using polls or box office numbers, YouTube allowed immediate, unfiltered reactions. A viewer felt **involved** in the creative process. They could

suggest improvements, request follow-up videos, or engage in debates with other commenters. Over time, certain comment sections became lively forums where users recognized one another's usernames and formed mini-communities.

3. **Rating and Discovery**
   - YouTube's rating system, though basic, helped the site display highly rated clips on the front page or category pages. This offered a type of **democratic curation**, where users' collective ratings determined which videos might gain more visibility. Early creators learned that producing content people wanted to rate highly could earn a spot on the front page, sometimes resulting in thousands of new viewers.

These interactions gave YouTube a lively, **community-focused identity**. Videos were not just posted and forgotten; they sparked conversations. People became willing to upload more content because they saw a responsive audience waiting on the other side of the screen.

3. Channel Pages and Subscriptions

As YouTube's user base expanded in 2005 and 2006, the founders realized they needed a better way for individuals to manage their own presence on the site. This led to the introduction of **channel pages**. While these were initially simple, they served an important role in helping users organize their videos and represent their online identity.

1. **Early Channel Page Features**
   - A channel page had a **username**, a **profile photo**, a list of **uploaded videos**, and sometimes a small text box for a personal introduction. Users could also see basic statistics like how many times a video was viewed, but advanced analytics tools did not exist yet.
   - Channel pages were publicly visible, so people could explore someone's entire collection of videos in one place. This made it easier to follow creators who posted vlogs, comedic sketches, or music covers regularly.
2. **The Subscribe Button**
   - One of the most significant early additions was a **Subscribe** button on each channel. If a viewer liked a creator's videos, they could subscribe to that channel to see new uploads in their personal "subscriptions" feed. This feed was a rudimentary version of what we now know as a content feed on many social platforms.
   - Subscribing was **free** and offered fans a chance to stay updated on their favorite creators' latest releases. Although the concept might seem obvious now, it was a huge leap forward at the time. It encouraged a continuous bond between viewers and uploaders, turning sporadic watchers into recurring community members.

3. **Building a Following**
   - As some channels gained more subscribers, their creators began feeling like they had a **fan base**—even if it was just a few hundred people. The community aspect blossomed when these creators began addressing their subscribers directly in videos, thanking them for support, or asking for topic suggestions.

- Early "vloggers" (video bloggers) in particular benefited from subscriptions. They would post regular updates on their personal lives, and viewers would tune in to watch each new chapter. This personal connection was a step away from mass-produced entertainment and closer to the concept of sharing stories among friends.

By letting viewers subscribe to channels they liked, YouTube built **consistent engagement**. It wasn't just about one viral clip; it was about returning to the site regularly to see what your favorite people had uploaded next. This model played a crucial role in sustaining the platform's growth and anchoring the community in ongoing relationships rather than one-off interactions.

4. Groups, Friend Lists, and Early Social Features

Though YouTube did not initially market itself as a "social network," the platform introduced features that nudged it in that direction. Groups, friend lists, and private messages gave users multiple ways to connect with each other beyond commenting on videos.

1. **User-Created Groups**
   - For a brief time in YouTube's early history, there was an option for **Groups**—user-created communities within the site. For example, fans of a certain TV show or a particular hobby (like guitar playing) could create a group page and invite others to join. Members could share videos on a common topic.
   - While this feature was not as prominent as channel subscriptions, it let niche communities form more easily. People who loved cooking, for instance, could gather in a group and swap cooking videos or tutorials. This feature gave a small glimpse of how YouTube might evolve into a network of specialized sub-communities.
2. **Friend Lists**
   - YouTube allowed users to add each other as "friends." Once accepted, you could view a "friends list" on your channel page. This was reminiscent of early social networks where being on someone's friend list was a casual way to indicate a closer connection.
   - Creators sometimes used friend lists to keep track of loyal fans or collaborators. Fans, on the other hand, might add their favorite creators to signal support or interest. Though these friend lists never reached the sophistication of dedicated social sites, they contributed to the feeling that YouTube was more than just a place to watch videos.
3. **Private Messaging**
   - **Private messaging** allowed users to communicate one-on-one without posting public comments. This enabled collaborations, invitations to group projects, or simple exchanges of ideas between creators and viewers. While some used it for friendly chats, others used it for more formal discussions about future projects.
   - This messaging system contributed to the growth of a real social fabric on YouTube. It was basic—no fancy layouts, no large attachments—but it got the job done, allowing personal connections to form behind the scenes.

Even though these early social features were not as robust as those found on specialized social networking sites, they nonetheless **encouraged bonding**. The notion that you could befriend someone whose videos you enjoyed, or collaborate via private messages, helped shape YouTube's identity as a community-driven platform where genuine relationships could develop.

5. Collaborations and Cross-Promotions

A pivotal aspect of community building on YouTube was the way creators teamed up to make videos together. These **collaborations** strengthened friendships, exposed creators to each other's audiences, and fueled a culture of sharing ideas.

1. **Early Collaborative Projects**
   - Sometimes two vloggers who lived in the same city might film a video together, engaging in a conversation or performing a skit. Fans of each vlogger would then discover the other, leading to a **cross-pollination** of audiences.
   - In other cases, collaborations were done virtually. One creator might record half a conversation and send the footage to another, who would then insert their part of the dialogue or reaction. While this process was more cumbersome, it often resulted in unique, split-screen videos that amazed viewers.
2. **Shout-Outs and Guest Appearances**
   - Creators learned that simply **mentioning** another channel in their video—known as a "shout-out"—could boost that channel's subscriber count. This was one of the earliest methods of **organic promotion** on YouTube.
   - Sometimes a popular creator invited a smaller creator to appear in a segment, giving the smaller channel significant exposure. These guest appearances built camaraderie and further advanced the sense that YouTube was a tight-knit community where established names helped newcomers.
3. **Community Challenges and Tag Games**
   - Another collaboration style involved "community challenges." A creator might issue a fun challenge—like filming yourself doing a certain dance—and then tag other creators to do the same. Those people would respond with their own videos, often tagging more users to keep the trend going.
   - This playful method connected strangers who shared a sense of humor or a hobby. Over time, tag games helped scatter interesting ideas across the platform. Entire series of videos formed around a single concept, each with a slightly different spin from a different creator.

Collaborations and cross-promotions played a huge role in weaving YouTube's early user base together. Rather than competing for views, many creators believed in **collective growth**. They saw that cooperation could lead to bigger audiences for everyone involved, which also made the site more attractive to viewers seeking varied content.

6. The Emergence of Niche Communities

As YouTube grew, users with highly specific interests started finding each other. This development gave rise to **niche communities**, each built around a shared passion.

1. **Examples of Early Niche Groups**
   - **Gaming**: Players uploaded recordings of their gameplay. Some provided commentary, discussing tips or reacting to in-game events. This was long before

"Let's Play" videos became a mainstream trend, so early gaming uploads felt like a secret club for enthusiasts.
    - **Beauty and Fashion**: Aspiring makeup artists showed off favorite products, offered tutorials, or shared daily routines. Viewers who searched for makeup tips discovered entire channels dedicated to the topic.
    - **Music Covers**: Amateur singers and instrumentalists uploaded videos of themselves performing well-known songs. Some gained small followings, especially if they performed unique renditions of popular hits.
2. **Focus on Community Interaction**
    - These groups formed **strong bonds**. A user who commented frequently on a beauty guru's videos might be recognized as a regular, leading to personal conversations. A gamer who specialized in a certain title could become known as an expert in that corner of the community.
    - **Collaboration** within each niche also emerged. Gamers might join forces to create multi-person gaming videos. Beauty creators might do "swap" videos, sending each other products and filming their reactions. Music channels might collaborate on cover mash-ups, merging instrumental and vocal parts.
3. **The Growth of Specialized Knowledge**
    - Because these communities developed organically, each niche had its own norms and insider terminology. For instance, gamers used game-specific jargon, while beauty channels formed a unique culture around product "hauls," where creators displayed new makeup items on camera.
    - Over time, these pockets of specialized knowledge attracted more viewers. People who felt isolated in real life because of a niche interest could find like-minded individuals on YouTube. This dynamic led to deeper community ties and encouraged more people to upload and share.

The rise of these smaller but dedicated communities underlined YouTube's role as a **platform for self-expression**. Unlike television, which catered to broad audiences, YouTube gave each niche the space to grow. This sense of belonging mattered greatly to early adopters, and it expanded the site's reputation as an inclusive place for any topic under the sun.

7. Fandom Culture and Early Creator Identities

By 2006, certain creators on YouTube had developed **loyal fan bases**, sometimes referred to as "fandoms." This phenomenon showcased how individual personalities were becoming a big draw on the platform.

1. **Vlogger Personalities**
    - Vloggers often talked about their daily lives, opinions, or experiences, building personal connections with viewers. Over time, fans got to know these individuals almost like friends. Some viewers left supportive comments or even fan art, reflecting how personal the connection felt.
    - Creators who revealed a lot about their personal lives sometimes found themselves with fans who felt deeply invested. While mostly positive, this could also bring challenges such as privacy concerns. Nonetheless, it highlighted that creators were not just random names on the internet—they were perceived as **authentic personalities**.
2. **Fan Meetups and Viewer Gatherings**

- In some cities, creators organized small, informal **meetups** where fans could come say hello. This was new territory—meeting an online video personality in person felt both exciting and novel.
- Early meetups were often quite casual—perhaps at a coffee shop or a public park. Over time, these gatherings grew in size, reflecting a new type of celebrity status that wasn't tied to Hollywood or mainstream media but to online engagement.

3. **Creator Branding and Identity**
    - Some creators began to develop **logos**, **catchphrases**, or consistent intros in their videos to establish a recognizable brand. They weren't part of large entertainment corporations; they were individuals creating personal brands from their bedrooms.
    - Fans would repeat these catchphrases in comments or wear T-shirts featuring a creator's channel name. This might seem small in scope at the time, but it indicated a shift: user-generated personalities were gaining influence similar to that of traditional celebrities—on a smaller, but still significant, scale.

This early fandom culture signaled that YouTube was moving beyond simply hosting videos. It was turning into an entertainment ecosystem where personalities emerged, fans rallied, and cultural references sprang up around these grassroots creators.

8. Community Guidelines and Content Moderation

As YouTube's community expanded, **moderation** became a key issue. The founders wanted to maintain the platform's openness but also needed rules to ensure user behavior didn't spiral out of control.

1. **Early Guidelines**
    - YouTube introduced **basic community guidelines** prohibiting explicit violence, nudity, hate speech, and other forms of offensive content. At first, these rules were brief statements, relying on users to flag violations. There wasn't a large dedicated moderation team.
    - The site also struggled with **copyrighted content**—users sometimes uploaded TV shows or music videos they didn't own. While that was largely handled under separate copyright policies, it intersected with broader moderation strategies.
2. **User Reports and Flagging**
    - To manage the growing volume of uploads, YouTube leaned heavily on **user flagging**. If a video violated guidelines or displayed inappropriate content, viewers could click a "flag" button to alert administrators.
    - This community-based moderation reflected YouTube's collaborative ethos but also introduced risks of misuse (such as false flagging out of dislike for a certain creator). Still, it was a necessary step to control harmful or prohibited material.
3. **Striving for Balance**
    - YouTube wanted to remain a **platform for free expression**, where everyday people could upload anything from daily vlogs to edgy comedy, as long as it wasn't harmful or illegal. But striking the right balance was difficult.
    - Some users felt that the guidelines restricted creativity, while others thought YouTube needed stricter rules. The founders had to figure out how to keep the platform safe and welcoming without becoming authoritarian. This tension remains a recurring theme in social media history.

Although the community guidelines were relatively simple in 2006, they established the basis for future enforcement. This was another sign that YouTube's culture of open exchange also required oversight, especially as it grew at an incredible pace.

9. The Impact of Early Partnerships on Community Building

During YouTube's early years, there were no formal "partner programs" like those that would arrive later, but smaller-scale partnerships and sponsorships began to pop up.

1. **Small Brand Sponsorships**
   - Certain creators formed informal deals with brands, receiving free products to review or wear in their videos. This was especially common in niche communities like beauty and fashion. The creator might say, "Company X sent me this item to try," and viewers would weigh in with opinions.
   - While not widespread, these small sponsorships hinted at an emerging structure where creators could benefit from making videos, beyond just receiving compliments from viewers. It also introduced **ethical questions** about disclosure, though no formal rules existed yet.
2. **Collaborative Promotions**
   - YouTube staff occasionally worked with small media producers to highlight unique or original content. For instance, an independent filmmaker might upload a short movie, and YouTube could feature it if it had enough creative flair.
   - These promotional efforts were not purely business deals but more about **building a vibrant library** of interesting videos. This, in turn, enriched the community. People who came to watch an indie short film might stay to check out comedic sketches from amateur creators, or vice versa.
3. **User Celebrations and Events**
   - Though not formal partnerships, YouTube sometimes promoted user-run events like "YouTube gatherings," where large groups of users from different niches would meet in a city to talk about video-making. These gatherings fostered **cross-community friendships**.
   - By endorsing or spotlighting these events on the official site blog, YouTube signaled that it valued user-led initiatives. This kept the overall community spirit strong and gave creators more reasons to stay active.

CHAPTER 8: THE RISE OF VIRAL VIDEOS

1. Introduction: Defining "Viral" in Early YouTube

In 2005 and 2006, the term "viral video" was not yet a mainstream phrase, but the concept was already in motion. A clip would be **shared rapidly** from person to person via email, instant messaging, MySpace embeds, and direct links, racking up tens or even hundreds of thousands of views in a short time. For a platform that was still new, such bursts of attention were remarkable and often unpredictable. One day, a video might be sitting at just a few hundred views; the next day, an unexpected wave of traffic could catapult it into the thousands.

In this chapter, we examine how certain early YouTube videos went "viral," how that virality shaped the platform's identity, and why these unexpected hits captivated the imaginations of both creators and viewers. We'll also see how mainstream media outlets started paying attention to these digital phenomena, giving YouTube a broader cultural impact than anyone initially anticipated.

2. The "Numa Numa" Phenomenon

One of the first major internet video sensations—often cited in discussions about YouTube's earliest viral hits—was **"Numa Numa,"** featuring a young man lip-syncing and dancing to the Romanian pop song "Dragostea Din Tei."

1. **Origins Outside YouTube**
    - Interestingly, "Numa Numa" first appeared on another website before making its way to YouTube, but it gained **much wider exposure** once it was uploaded to YouTube's user-friendly platform.
    - The clip showed a regular individual gleefully mouthing the words of a foreign pop tune while performing exaggerated arm movements in front of his computer. Its charm was its raw, unpolished spontaneity.
2. **Spreading Through Email and Blogs**
    - Friends emailed the link to one another, calling it "hilarious" or "random." Bloggers embedded or shared the YouTube link, introducing the video to new circles of viewers. Because watching it required no special software beyond a web browser, the barrier to sharing was low.
    - This comedic, earnest performance resonated with the early YouTube culture: ordinary people doing entertaining things in their personal spaces, free from big production budgets or corporate oversight.
3. **Cultural Significance**
    - "Numa Numa" went on to inspire many **imitations**. Other users recreated the dance or added their own comedic twists. People in different parts of the world recognized the catchy tune and joined the trend.
    - The video also grabbed mainstream media attention. News outlets occasionally referenced it as an example of how the internet could make an average person famous overnight. This was a **turning point**—people began realizing that a single clip on YouTube could reach a global audience far beyond someone's immediate circle of friends.

Though not the only viral hit of its time, "Numa Numa" stood out as a perfect illustration of YouTube's capacity to amplify personal, spontaneous moments. It hinted at a future where creativity and humor, regardless of professional polish, could travel instantly across the world.

3. "Charlie Bit My Finger" and Kids in Viral Content

Another pivotal viral clip was **"Charlie Bit My Finger,"** featuring two young British brothers in a brief but endearing sibling moment. The older brother places his finger in Charlie's mouth, and Charlie bites down. It's an everyday family scene, but it became a global sensation once it landed on YouTube.

1. **Simplicity and Universal Appeal**
    - The video is less than a minute long, featuring a simple, relatable event—kids being silly and adorable. The older brother's playful complaint ("Ouch, Charlie!") combined with the toddler's reaction made viewers around the world laugh.
    - Because no complex language or cultural references were needed, the clip **transcended language barriers**, appealing to viewers in many countries.
2. **Rapid Sharing Across Social Circles**
    - Friends emailed the link, families watched it together, and bloggers posted it under titles like "Cutest thing ever" or "You have to see this!" In a short span, the view count soared to hundreds of thousands, then millions—an enormous number for YouTube's early days.
    - Reactions in the comments section ranged from "That's so cute!" to comedic exaggerations. Some people even created **remixes** or edited versions. This was one of the first widely known examples of the "remix culture" that would later become prominent on YouTube.
3. **Impact on the Family**
    - The family behind "Charlie Bit My Finger" discovered a strange kind of internet fame. Their kids became recognized around the world, and the phrase "Ouch, Charlie" turned into a catchphrase among viewers.
    - Though they did not initially intend to monetize or capitalize on the video, the massive attention hinted at the potential for **family-friendly content**. This shift underscored how ordinary people could stumble into online celebrity status just by sharing a fleeting moment.

"Charlie Bit My Finger" demonstrated that YouTube was not only about comedic sketches, lip-syncing, or stunts. **Everyday life**—especially involving kids or pets—could resonate deeply, proving that the simplest moments sometimes generated the biggest waves.

4. The "Evolution of Dance" and the Comedy/Dance Craze

In 2006, a comedian named Judson Laipply uploaded a performance called **"Evolution of Dance."** He mashed together iconic dance moves from different decades, all set to a medley of pop songs. Filmed at a live event, this clip soon exploded in popularity on YouTube.

1. **Performance with a Twist**
   - The act featured Laipply running through dance styles from Elvis-era rock and roll to modern hip-hop. It was both **funny** and **nostalgic**, appealing to viewers who recognized the songs and moves.
   - The camera work was basic, reflecting that it was likely recorded for personal archives. Still, the performance's charm and unique concept made it **instantly shareable**.
2. **Media Coverage and Rapid Climb**
   - Mainstream news outlets wrote articles about "Evolution of Dance," describing how a single comedic performance racked up millions of views. For the time, those numbers were massive.
   - Because the clip contained well-known songs, it also sparked discussions about copyright on YouTube. Nevertheless, for a while it remained online, racking up attention at a rate rarely seen before. Some called it the **most-viewed YouTube video** at that point, highlighting how fast something could go viral.
3. **Inspiring Similar Videos**
   - Countless users tried to mimic the "Evolution of Dance" concept, creating their own compilations of popular moves and songs. Some did comedic twists; others highlighted cultural or regional dances.
   - This wave of copycat content pointed to a **new phenomenon**: if one video rose to fame, many others would follow, each attempting to catch the same wave of interest. This was beneficial for building the site's overall library, but it also introduced competition among creators eager to replicate someone else's success.

The explosion of "Evolution of Dance" showed that a unique idea performed in a spirited way could spread like wildfire on YouTube. This phenomenon underscored the platform's power: an **unknown comedian** could become an internet sensation, purely through grassroots sharing and the inherent entertainment value of his act.

5. Celebrity Lip Syncs and Unexpected Star Power

Another style of viral video that popped up in YouTube's earliest days involved **lip sync performances**. Sometimes they featured everyday people lip-syncing to popular songs, but occasionally real celebrities joined the fun, albeit unintentionally at first.

1. **Homemade Lip Sync Trends**
   - Many users recorded themselves miming the words to radio hits. Some did it alone, others in groups. The casual, in-bedroom setting gave these videos a certain charm, reminiscent of kids singing into hairbrushes.
   - When viewers stumbled across a lip sync they found particularly funny or well-executed, they shared it with friends. These videos were easy to reproduce, so more and more people tried their hand at it.
2. **Accidental Celebrity Moments**
   - Sometimes a celebrity would appear in a clip that wasn't meant for public consumption, only for it to be uploaded to YouTube. For instance, behind-the-scenes footage of actors or musicians goofing off might surface.
   - Though these leaks were not always welcomed by the celebrities, they contributed to YouTube's **reputation as a place for candid content**. Fans relished seeing big names in casual, unguarded moments, even if the original purpose was never to go public.
3. **Late-Night Hosts and Early Talk Shows**
   - A few talk show hosts recognized the viral potential of lip sync segments. They began integrating them into their programs, posting the snippets on YouTube afterward. While the major push for talk show integration came later, these early seeds showed the potential synergy between traditional media and the platform.
   - As a result, some videos that appeared on late-night TV found a second life on YouTube, generating even more views than their broadcast audience.

Lip sync videos—whether by everyday users or unintentional celebrity appearances—further demonstrated YouTube's **crossover appeal**. Ordinary people could mimic big stars, and big stars occasionally showed up in casual or leaked footage, creating a feedback loop that fueled more viewer interest in comedic or musical videos.

6. The Role of Traditional Media in Boosting Viral Clips

Mainstream media began to notice YouTube's viral hits, referencing them on TV, radio, and in newspaper articles. This coverage turned a big spotlight onto YouTube, driving curious viewers to the site.

1. **News Segments Highlighting Viral Videos**
   - Morning shows and entertainment news programs often aired short segments on "what's hot online," spotlighting a particular YouTube clip that had gained popularity.
   - These mentions on traditional media had a compounding effect: People who weren't active internet users suddenly heard about a silly dance or a cute baby video and felt compelled to look it up. That meant more visits to YouTube, which pushed the view counts even higher.
2. **Talk Show Interviews with Viral Stars**
   - On rare occasions, a creator of a viral clip was invited to appear on a national talk show. Interviewers asked them how the video was made, why they posted it, and how they felt about becoming famous overnight.
   - These interviews sometimes generated more viral interest because viewers at home got to see the backstory of the clip. They then rushed online to watch or re-watch the video, leaving comments like "I saw you on TV!"
3. **Early Recognition of YouTube as a Media Disruptor**
   - Some journalists began to discuss YouTube as a **potential disruptor** to traditional media. If random home videos could captivate millions, what did that mean for the future of television?
   - While not everyone saw YouTube as an outright replacement for TV, many acknowledged that user-generated content was now competing, at least in terms of viewer attention. Media companies took notice, leading to a mix of collaborations and legal tussles down the line.

This interaction with traditional media was crucial for YouTube's early growth. Viral hits were no longer confined to internet-savvy circles. They broke into mainstream awareness, making YouTube a household name much faster than if it had stayed within online communities alone.

7. Reaction Videos and the Emergence of Internet Memes

By late 2006, a new type of content began to flourish on YouTube: **reaction videos**. In these, people filmed themselves watching or responding to something—often another viral clip. Meanwhile, "memes" started forming around repeated ideas or jokes that circulated in various forms.

1. **Watching People Watch Videos**
   - Reaction videos were intriguing because they captured genuine responses—laughter, shock, excitement—in real time. For viewers, it felt like **watching a friend** experience the same funny or surprising moments.
   - This format promoted a **chain reaction** of engagement. One viral clip could spawn numerous reaction videos, each amassing its own audience. This further spread the original content.
2. **Birth of Internet Memes on YouTube**
   - Memes are cultural symbols or ideas that replicate as people share and add their own twists. YouTube enabled memes to spread visually and audibly, rather than just through text or images.
   - For example, a short sound clip from a viral video might get repeated, remixed, and turned into a catchphrase. A comedic dance move might become a meme as various users replicated or exaggerated it. This iterative culture flourished on YouTube, where copying and remixing were as easy as uploading a short clip.
3. **Community Participation**
   - Memes and reaction videos heavily relied on **community participation**. Viewers didn't just watch; they also contributed their own versions or posted feedback.
   - This participatory spirit strengthened YouTube's identity as a creative sandbox. While some critics dismissed memes as frivolous, they played a huge role in fueling user engagement and fun, ensuring that the community had fresh material to keep it active.

Through reaction videos and meme culture, YouTube demonstrated its ability to **evolve rapidly**. Popular videos no longer existed in isolation. They became foundations for other kinds of content, making the platform a constantly shifting tapestry of shared jokes and references.

8. The Community's Impact on Viral Spread

The success of viral videos on YouTube wasn't just a result of random luck. It stemmed from an engaged user community that actively promoted clips they found compelling, funny, or shocking.

1. **Comment Sections as Hype Engines**
    - When a video started to gain traction, the comment section often buzzed with exclamations like "This is hilarious!" or "Everyone needs to see this!" Some users posted direct links to other social platforms, inviting even more outsiders to watch.
    - This environment functioned like **word-of-mouth marketing** in a digital space. If enough people exclaimed that a video was must-see content, a bigger wave of viewers inevitably followed.
2. **Embedding and Email Sharing**
    - Besides direct views on the YouTube website, **embeds** on personal blogs or MySpace pages amplified exposure. Email shares also played a key role in an era when messaging apps were not as widespread as they are today.
    - People would simply copy the video link and paste it into an email with a subject line like "Check out this hilarious clip!" Once the email was opened, the recipient could click and instantly watch, no sign-ups required.
3. **Viewer Ownership**
    - A sense of **ownership** developed among early adopters who discovered a video "before it was cool." They loved being the ones to show it to friends first. This social dynamic spurred individuals to share widely.
    - Because YouTube had no paywalls or complicated steps, the friction to watch was minimal. Users felt a certain pride in helping a deserving video get more attention. In that way, the community itself became a driving force in the viral cycle.

Collectively, these behaviors made the community a central mechanism in how and why a video went viral. The user-centric design, combined with easy sharing tools, meant that the audience acted as both **consumers** and **promoters**, all but guaranteeing that engaging or quirky content could blow up almost overnight.

9. Advertising and Brand-Driven Viral Attempts

Though most early viral videos were personal or comedic in nature, a few **brands** realized that they could harness the viral effect. Businesses experimented with making short ads or comedic sketches, hoping they would spread as naturally as user-generated content.

1. **Sneaky Ads Disguised as Regular Clips**
    - Some companies produced "stealth marketing" videos that resembled user-generated content. For instance, a supposed "prank" video might secretly be staged and sponsored by a soda brand.
    - Reactions to these tactics were mixed. If viewers discovered the corporate intent, they often accused the company of being dishonest. Still, a few brand-driven clips managed to spread widely before the public realized they were ads.
2. **Openly Branded Viral Tries**
    - Other businesses were more upfront about their involvement, posting short, humorous commercials. Some gained traction if they were genuinely entertaining.
    - While these branded videos seldom reached the level of purely organic hits, they showed marketers that YouTube held massive potential for **viral advertising**.
3. **User Response to Brand Content**
    - The YouTube community valued authenticity. Many users were skeptical of anything that smelled too corporate. However, if an ad was **funny, unique, or relatable**, viewers might still share it, as happened with some "fake movie trailers" or comedic campaigns.
    - This tension between user-generated authenticity and corporate interest foreshadowed future debates about balancing community culture with commercialization on YouTube.

Early brand attempts at virality proved that YouTube was not just a playground for amateurs but also a potential goldmine for **marketing**. However, success required understanding what appealed to everyday users and why they chose to pass a video along. Too much overt branding could backfire, while subtle creativity sometimes thrived.

CHAPTER 9: EARLY CHALLENGES AND COMPETITORS

1. Introduction: YouTube's Rising Pressure

By late 2005 and throughout 2006, YouTube was on a rapid upward trajectory. Each month brought new users, more video uploads, and greater public awareness. But with success came serious **challenges**. On the technical side, the site demanded ever-increasing bandwidth and server capacity to keep up with the rush of uploads and views. Financially, the young startup had to secure funding to cover these rising costs. Meanwhile, on the competitive front, several other video-sharing platforms wanted a piece of the emerging market.

In this chapter, we will look at the obstacles YouTube encountered in its early history, including issues with bandwidth, worries about monetization, and user retention. We will also examine the most notable **rivals** YouTube faced—both established tech giants and smaller ventures that offered video-sharing services. Understanding how YouTube tackled these hurdles provides insight into the determination and creativity that helped the company establish itself as the primary platform for user-generated video content.

2. The Bandwidth Crisis: Strain on Infrastructure

2.1. Exponential Growth in Traffic

From the moment YouTube left its beta phase, user engagement soared. Videos that had a few hundred views one day could jump into the tens of thousands the next if they went viral or got embedded on a popular blog. Each view demanded data transfer from YouTube's servers to the viewer's computer, and each upload required permanent storage space. The result was a **continuous surge** in bandwidth usage and disk space consumption.

For a small startup, these demands were daunting. While standard web hosting might handle simple content like text or images, **streaming video** required a robust infrastructure that was far more expensive. The founders and their engineers found themselves in a cycle: the more popular YouTube became, the more it cost to keep it running smoothly.

2.2. Trying to Keep the Service Stable

Maintaining **site stability** became a primary focus in YouTube's early days. Crashes or downtime were frequent concerns, especially when a highly shared video drew thousands of simultaneous viewers. Early employees scrambled to add servers, balance traffic loads, and optimize how videos were delivered.

Steve Chen, one of YouTube's co-founders, spent countless hours refining the platform's backend. As usage grew, they had to adopt more advanced **content delivery methods**, distributing videos across multiple data centers to minimize latency. Even so, it was not unusual for users to experience brief slowdowns or buffering during peak traffic times. These hiccups were part of YouTube's **growing pains**, as the platform scaled at a pace few startups had ever seen.

2.3. The Financial Burden

Paying for high-volume bandwidth was a constant challenge. Even with venture capital funding from firms like Sequoia Capital, the bills for data transfer arrived monthly, and they were huge. The company needed these investments just to break even on operational costs.

At times, the YouTube team worried that they might have to limit upload sizes or restrict viewing options. But such moves risked stifling the very growth they depended on. Instead, the founders chose to **push forward**, confident that they could find new funding sources or partnerships that would keep the site alive. Their willingness to prioritize user experience—ensuring that uploading remained free and unconstrained—proved key to YouTube's success, even if it meant running on razor-thin margins for a while.

3. Monetization Worries: How to Pay the Bills

3.1. Early Advertising Attempts

In YouTube's first year, the founders tested **banner ads** or small advertisements placed around the video player. While these ads brought in some revenue, it was nowhere close to covering the ballooning costs of bandwidth. Also, many users and staff felt that intrusive ads clashed with YouTube's grassroots, community-centric feel.

The platform had no robust system for **in-video advertising** at the time. Pre-roll or mid-roll ads were almost nonexistent, largely because the technology and user expectations weren't ready. Most viewers associated online video ads with clunky experiences. The founders feared that pushing video ads too soon might drive users away.

3.2. Dependence on Venture Capital

Because ad revenue remained minimal, YouTube leaned heavily on investor money. Each new funding round had to be justified with user growth metrics and projections of future profitability. Investors saw potential in YouTube—thousands of sign-ups, millions of daily views—but also recognized the risk. Could YouTube eventually turn its massive user base into actual profit?

For the founders, the immediate priority was to **establish dominance** in the user-generated video space. They believed that if YouTube captured enough market share, they would figure out monetization later—either through innovative ad strategies or by merging with a larger tech company. This forward-looking approach kept YouTube afloat, but the lack of a proven business model led critics to question whether the company was chasing "eyeballs" at the expense of sustainable revenue.

3.3. Debates Over Premium Services

Inside YouTube, some discussions arose about **premium features**—charging users for faster uploads, higher video quality, or advanced analytics. But the site's identity was strongly tied to being free and open. Adding a paywall ran the risk of alienating the audience that made YouTube popular in the first place.

Ultimately, the team decided not to move forward with premium services during these early years. They believed user growth and brand-building were more important than short-term revenue. This strategy proved wise in the long run, as YouTube's enormous user base would later drive interest from major industry players, including Google.

4. Facing Early Rivals in the Video-Sharing Space

4.1. Dailymotion, Metacafe, and Vimeo

During YouTube's meteoric rise, several competitors emerged or already existed, hoping to claim a slice of the user-generated video market:

- **Dailymotion**: Founded in France in 2005, Dailymotion offered a similar approach to uploading and sharing videos. It attracted a European audience but struggled to match YouTube's rapid user growth in the United States.

- **Metacafe**: This site gained traction by focusing on short, entertaining clips—especially homegrown videos and user-generated humor. Metacafe also experimented with revenue-sharing for creators at an earlier stage than YouTube.

- **Vimeo**: Created in 2004, Vimeo appealed to more artistic users. Its design and community guidelines emphasized high-quality videos and a certain aesthetic. Early on, Vimeo catered to a niche group of filmmakers and creatives, so it did not compete directly with YouTube's mainstream appeal, but it was still a recognized alternative.

While each of these platforms had unique features, none matched YouTube's explosive scale. YouTube's **simple upload system**, strong community vibe, and early success with viral content gave it a clear edge. Even so, these sites carved out their own user bases, forcing YouTube to keep improving lest it lose ground to a focused rival.

4.2. Revver and Revenue Sharing

Another notable competitor was **Revver**, which launched around the same time. Revver tried a **creator-friendly** model, placing ads at the end of videos and splitting revenue with content producers. Some believed this approach was more attractive to serious video makers looking to earn money from their work.

However, Revver never gained the widespread popularity YouTube enjoyed. The user base was smaller, and the lure of earning a bit of ad revenue wasn't enough to overcome YouTube's massive audience advantage. Creators who wanted exposure found that YouTube's community of millions was more valuable than a smaller potential payday on another platform.

4.3. Why YouTube Pulled Ahead

Several factors helped YouTube outdistance its rivals:

1. **User-Friendly Interface**: While some competitors had advanced features, they often felt more complicated. YouTube's straightforward design and Flash-based playback were accessible to the average internet user.

2. **Viral Culture**: YouTube became the go-to spot for memes, comedic sketches, and everyday life clips that could skyrocket in popularity. This culture of viral sharing brought in waves of new viewers.

3. **Community Engagement**: Ratings, comments, and subscriptions encouraged people to stay active on the site. Alternative platforms sometimes lacked these robust community features or did not promote them as effectively.

4. **Early Momentum**: YouTube's brand name quickly became synonymous with online video, making it a first choice for new uploaders, especially in the United States.

By late 2006, YouTube's lead in the user-generated video arena was so large that most rivals aimed for niche audiences. This first-mover advantage, combined with consistent press coverage, gave YouTube the power to shape the conversation around online video.

5. The Threat from Social Media Giants

5.1. MySpace and Its Video Features

In the mid-2000s, **MySpace** was a massive social networking site, with tens of millions of users who loved customizing profile pages and posting music. Recognizing the popularity of video content, MySpace added its own video section. The site hoped to keep users from venturing to YouTube for their video needs.

However, MySpace Video had limitations. It often took a long time to process uploads, and it was overshadowed by MySpace's core feature of music discovery. In contrast, YouTube's entire focus was video, giving it a more direct path to innovation in that space.

5.2. Facebook's Emergence

In 2005 and 2006, **Facebook** was still mostly a college-focused network. It had not yet become the worldwide giant it is now. Video features on Facebook were minimal. Users primarily posted photos, text status updates, and used the platform's "poke" function. Nevertheless, some industry watchers speculated that if Facebook adopted robust video tools, it might challenge YouTube by merging video with a social graph of real-life friends.

At this stage, though, Facebook was not a major threat in the video realm. It would take several more years for Facebook to introduce stronger video capabilities. During YouTube's early rise, the main pressure came not from social networks but from smaller video platforms scrambling to replicate YouTube's success.

5.3. The Embedding Advantage

Ironically, MySpace inadvertently boosted YouTube. Because YouTube allowed **easy embedding**, MySpace users often inserted YouTube clips into their MySpace profiles. This synergy drove huge view counts back to YouTube, which soared in popularity among MySpace's massive user base.

Had MySpace disabled or restricted these embeds, it might have curtailed YouTube's viral reach. But MySpace was reluctant to anger its users, who enjoyed customizing their pages with YouTube videos. Thus, YouTube remained an **essential tool** for social sharing, which contributed significantly to its dominance.

6. Cultural Skepticism and Mainstream Doubts

6.1. Critiques from Traditional Media

Even as YouTube garnered attention for its user-generated content, many traditional media executives saw it as a **passing fad**. They questioned the quality of user videos, viewing them as amateurish and lacking professional polish. Some predicted that the novelty of "funny homemade clips" would fade quickly.

Additionally, major broadcasting networks worried about **copyright abuses**, seeing YouTube as a potential hub for piracy. This skepticism delayed partnerships that could have benefited both parties. While younger audiences flocked to YouTube's authentic vibe, traditional media took a more cautious stance.

6.2. Doubts About Sustainability

Critics also doubted whether user-generated content could sustain viewers' long-term interest. They pointed to the ephemeral nature of viral hits, claiming that once the "shock" or novelty wore off, people would return to mainstream TV shows and films.

Moreover, the lack of a clear profit model fueled speculation that YouTube might flame out like other dot-com ventures. Experts recalled the **dot-com bust** of the early 2000s, where many internet startups vanished after failing to generate revenue. They warned that YouTube's high operational costs, combined with limited income, placed it in a precarious position.

6.3. The Company's Response

YouTube's founders acknowledged these concerns but believed that the internet was evolving toward more **user-driven platforms**. They pointed out that blogging and photo-sharing sites had also faced skepticism, only to become central parts of everyday internet usage.

Internally, the team remained focused on **refining the user experience**, believing that if they could maintain a loyal and growing community, the rest would fall into place. This faith in the power of user engagement—and the speed at which viral content could make an impact—kept YouTube pushing forward despite external doubts.

7. Internal Growing Pains: Team Expansion and Culture

7.1. Rapid Hiring

As YouTube expanded, so did its staff. New engineers were needed to optimize video streaming and storage, while more customer support specialists handled user inquiries and flagged videos. Marketers and partnership managers joined to explore potential deals with media outlets or advertisers.

This **quick hiring** spree led to classic startup challenges: training new employees, maintaining consistent goals, and preserving the company's culture. Some early staffers worried that too many hires might dilute the scrappy, "all-hands-on-deck" spirit that helped YouTube grow so fast.

7.2. Balancing Freedom and Focus

A significant part of YouTube's success was its **open, flexible environment**. Ideas could emerge from anyone—engineers, support staff, or the founders themselves—and be tested rapidly. But as the team scaled, leadership had to maintain a sense of focus. They introduced more formal processes for product decisions, ensuring that new features aligned with core needs rather than personal pet projects.

This tension between creative freedom and structured focus is common in startups transitioning from small teams to larger organizations. YouTube's leadership tried to keep bureaucracy to a minimum, encouraging employees to voice ideas. The goal was to remain **agile** and user-centric while setting priorities to address pressing issues like bandwidth, site stability, and community moderation.

7.3. Morale in a High-Pressure Environment

Surging usage was a "good problem" to have, but it meant the team was constantly dealing with potential system failures and unexpected traffic spikes. Employees often worked long hours, especially engineers who were on-call for server emergencies at night or over weekends.

On the plus side, each time a new viral video took off, staff felt a sense of shared excitement. Everyone understood they were building something with real cultural impact. This sense of mission and pride in the product helped offset the stress of rapid growth. Team morale was generally high, even amid uncertainties about how the site would eventually turn a profit.

8. Public Image Versus Competitors

8.1. Becoming Synonymous with Online Video

By late 2006, YouTube had a cultural cachet that none of its competitors could match. The phrase "I'll watch it on YouTube" became a common response to missing a funny moment on TV or wanting to see a music video. While other platforms existed, they did not capture the public's imagination in the same way.

Competitors tried different marketing strategies—emphasizing higher video quality, revenue sharing, or curated content—but YouTube's name recognition and massive user base gave it a **network effect**. The more people used YouTube, the more new users joined, because that was where all their friends were sharing videos.

8.2. Building Trust with Users

Another advantage for YouTube was a **trust factor**. Early users found the site easy to navigate and rarely faced significant technical hurdles. By comparison, sites that demanded special software downloads or forced registration before watching a clip felt less accessible.

Because YouTube had few barriers to entry, it attracted novices and enthusiasts alike. By the time a competitor came up with a new feature—such as better video quality—YouTube's established community and brand loyalty made it difficult for the rival to lure users away. The "YouTube habit" was deeply ingrained among content creators and viewers, who appreciated the synergy of uploading, subscribing, and discovering viral hits in one familiar place.

9. The "Utube.com" Confusion

9.1. A Surprising Legal Skirmish

One lesser-known challenge YouTube faced was **brand confusion** over the domain name. A company called **Universal Tube & Rollform Equipment Corporation** owned the domain "utube.com," which many internet users mistakenly typed when trying to reach "youtube.com." Traffic to utube.com spiked, causing the manufacturer's website to crash or run slowly.

Frustrated, Universal Tube filed a lawsuit against YouTube in late 2006, claiming that the sudden flood of misdirected users and the confusion over domain names harmed its business. Universal Tube even changed its site to "utubeonline.com" to manage the traffic problem.

9.2. Resolution of the Domain Issue

While this legal spat never reached the magnitude of YouTube's bigger copyright battles, it highlighted how the site's popularity could create unforeseen conflicts. The suit was eventually dismissed, but not without drawing media attention. Many found it amusing, though the situation caused genuine trouble for the metal tube manufacturer.

Ultimately, "utube.com" pivoted to a simple landing page explaining the confusion. The incident underscored the power of brand identity. YouTube had become so well-known that even a similar domain name caused floods of accidental visitors. This small scuffle revealed a side effect of rapid fame—sometimes, your brand can overshadow unrelated businesses that share part of your name.

CHAPTER 10: LEGAL BATTLES AND CONTROVERSIES

1. Introduction: The Shadow of Copyright and Content Control

From its inception, YouTube promoted **user freedom** to upload almost any kind of video—home movies, vlogs, skits, or short creative films. This approach, while integral to its success, exposed the platform to a flood of **copyrighted and potentially infringing content**. Music videos, TV show clips, and entire segments of movies made their way onto the site, often uploaded without permission. By 2006 and early 2007, YouTube's explosive growth attracted the attention of powerful media companies worried about lost revenue and unauthorized public distribution of their intellectual property.

In this chapter, we explore the **legal battles and controversies** that emerged during YouTube's early years. We will see how the platform grappled with demands from copyright holders, the introduction of formal takedown procedures, and broader ethical or social issues that surfaced as user-generated content sometimes went astray. These disputes tested YouTube's stance on free expression and posed existential questions about the balance between user empowerment and legal compliance.

2. The DMCA: A Framework for Takedowns

2.1. The Basics of the DMCA

The **Digital Millennium Copyright Act (DMCA)**, enacted in the United States in 1998, provided a **legal framework** for dealing with online copyright infringement. Under the DMCA, internet service providers and platform hosts could avoid liability if they promptly removed copyrighted material after receiving a valid takedown notice from the rightsholder. This principle was known as the **"Safe Harbor"** provision.

YouTube quickly integrated a **DMCA takedown process** into its operations. When a content owner discovered an infringing upload, they could file a complaint with YouTube.

2.2. The Takedown Process in Practice

Under the DMCA's "Safe Harbor" clause, platforms like YouTube had to respond **quickly and effectively** whenever a valid copyright complaint arrived. In practice, this process worked as follows:

1. **Complaint Submission**: A rightsholder—such as a TV network, movie studio, or record label—would send YouTube a **formal notification** that a specific video infringed upon their copyrighted material. This notice had to include certain details, like the precise URL of the video and the signature of the complaining party.
2. **Review and Removal**: Once YouTube received the notice, it would **verify** whether the complaint met the DMCA's requirements. If valid, YouTube typically removed the video from its site to avoid liability. In some cases, the alleged infringer could file a **counter-notification** disputing the claim, but most of the time, flagged content was simply taken down and stayed down.
3. **Repeat Infringers**: YouTube faced a challenge in dealing with users who repeatedly uploaded infringing content. The DMCA required "repeat infringer policies," so if a user's channel was flagged multiple times for legitimate copyright violations, YouTube could **terminate** the account to preserve its Safe Harbor protection.

Although the DMCA gave YouTube a legal blueprint, **carrying out** takedowns at the speed and volume required was daunting. By 2006, YouTube was receiving numerous copyright complaints daily—eventually ballooning into the thousands. The company scrambled to **automate** parts of the process while hiring teams to handle the more complicated issues manually.

2.3. Early Friction with Content Creators

During these early years, YouTube also dealt with **confusion** and **tension** among smaller content creators who worried their legitimate videos might be taken down unfairly:

- **False Positives**: Because copyright owners sometimes over-claimed materials (either by mistake or to err on the side of caution), legitimate content—like a creator's original music—could be removed if it resembled copyrighted tracks.

- **Fair Use Disputes**: U.S. copyright law allows "fair use" for commentary, criticism, parody, and other transformative works. However, YouTube often erred on the side of caution and took down videos upon receiving a takedown notice, leaving it up to users to file counter-notices. This led to complaints that YouTube was **too quick** to remove content without verifying actual infringement.

In these ways, the DMCA system was **imperfect**: it protected YouTube from massive liability but sometimes removed legitimate user-generated videos. Nonetheless, Safe Harbor was essential for a platform of YouTube's size and ambition. It allowed YouTube to host millions of uploads without pre-screening each clip—a task that would have been practically impossible.

3. Early High-Profile Lawsuits and Disputes

3.1. Universal Music Group and Warner Music Complaints

Music videos emerged as a central **flashpoint** in YouTube's early legal challenges. Popular recording artists, from major labels like Universal Music Group and Warner Music, often found their songs or music videos uploaded in full by fans. Record labels argued that this caused **loss of revenue**, as viewers no longer needed to buy tracks or watch official channels.

- **Takedown Tsunami**: In mid-2006, major labels sent an onslaught of DMCA takedown notices to YouTube. Thousands of music clips vanished from the site in a short period, stirring frustration among users who had shared or remixed those tracks out of fandom rather than profit.

- **Negotiation Attempts**: Behind the scenes, YouTube's founders tried to **strike licensing deals** with certain record labels, hoping to legitimize user uploads and possibly share advertising revenue. But the negotiations were complicated—labels wanted strong control over their catalogs and a share of potential ad earnings. YouTube, meanwhile, was still refining how to monetize.

Despite these tensions, some labels recognized YouTube's promotional potential. A song that went viral on YouTube could spark new interest and lead to album sales. This **push-pull dynamic** between fear of piracy and recognition of viral marketing underpinned many of the early disputes with the music industry.

3.2. TV Networks and Movie Studios

While music labels were among the loudest voices, **television networks** and **movie studios** also worried about piracy on YouTube. Clips of popular shows—sometimes entire episodes—appeared shortly after they aired. Movie scenes were similarly posted, occasionally in multiple parts.

- **NBC and the "Lazy Sunday" Incident**: One famous controversy involved a "Saturday Night Live" sketch called "Lazy Sunday," which gained significant traction on YouTube. Users uploaded the skit multiple times, and it became a viral sensation—even boosting SNL's profile among younger viewers. However, NBC initially demanded takedowns, concerned about losing control of its content.
- **Mixed Feelings**: As with the music industry, some TV executives noticed that viral sketches could **raise viewership**. NBC, for instance, later decided to upload some official segments to YouTube. This inconsistent approach—sometimes removing content, sometimes embracing it—reflected an industry grappling with new forms of online distribution.

Movie studios generally took a **tougher stance**, worried that users would leak entire films or spoil crucial scenes. Although full-length movie uploads were relatively rare (due to file size and length limits), short clips still raised concerns about partial piracy. YouTube had to work diligently to remove flagged content, walking a fine line between respecting copyright and maintaining user goodwill.

3.3. The Viacom Lawsuit: A Defining Moment

Among all the legal challenges YouTube faced, none was as significant or as widely publicized as the lawsuit filed by **Viacom** in March 2007. Viacom owned major networks like MTV, Comedy Central, and Nickelodeon, along with popular shows such as "The Daily Show" and "South Park."

1. **Lawsuit Details**
    - Viacom accused YouTube of **massive copyright infringement**, claiming that YouTube profited from the unauthorized uploads of thousands of Viacom-owned clips. The company demanded over **$1 billion** in damages, making it one of the largest internet-related lawsuits at the time.
2. **Allegations**
    - Viacom argued that YouTube was **willfully blind** to infringements. They claimed YouTube didn't do enough to remove infringing content quickly, thus benefiting from increased traffic.
    - YouTube countered that it followed the DMCA's takedown rules, removing clips promptly when notified. It insisted that the DMCA shielded them from liability as long as they complied in good faith.
3. **Public Reaction**
    - The lawsuit attracted extensive media coverage, pitting a traditional media powerhouse against a fast-growing tech platform.
    - Many users sided with YouTube, viewing Viacom's demands as excessive. Critics argued that large media corporations were trying to smother innovative platforms rather than find **mutually beneficial** solutions.
4. **Long Legal Saga**
    - The case dragged on for years, eventually leading to various rulings and appeals. Early on, a U.S. District Court sided with YouTube, citing DMCA Safe Harbor protection. Viacom appealed, and the back-and-forth continued until a final settlement in 2014, **long after** YouTube had become part of Google.
    - Although the ultimate settlement was confidential, the outcome largely **validated** YouTube's stance that it was not liable for every piece of user-uploaded content, as long as it followed DMCA procedures.

The Viacom lawsuit became a **symbol** of the clash between traditional media giants and emerging internet platforms. It also underscored how essential DMCA Safe Harbor was for websites that allowed user-generated content. Had Viacom won decisively, it might have forced YouTube—or similar platforms—to adopt far stricter upload filters or face crippling damages, fundamentally changing the open nature of online video sharing.

4. Content Policy Controversies Beyond Copyright

4.1. Offensive or Adult Material

From its earliest days, YouTube confronted issues of **inappropriate content**. While the site's guidelines forbade sexually explicit videos, graphic violence, and hate speech, **enforcement** was challenging. Some users tested the boundaries by uploading content that skirted or directly violated these rules.

- **Manual and Automated Review**: YouTube began experimenting with automated detection systems for nudity or extreme violence, but the technology was rudimentary. They relied heavily on **community flagging**—users reporting content that broke the rules.

- **Free Speech vs. Moderation**: The tension lay in deciding what to remove and what to leave up. One user's idea of offensive content might be another's creative expression. YouTube, wanting to foster an open environment, generally took down only material clearly violating the guidelines.

Still, these controversies occasionally spurred negative press, as critics argued YouTube wasn't doing enough to prevent minors from stumbling across adult or violent videos. The company responded by adding age-restriction features and stepping up manual review of flagged content.

4.2. Violent or Extremist Content

Another major concern was **extremist propaganda** and violent footage. Early on, extremist groups realized they could upload messages or disturbing content, counting on the site's broad reach. YouTube responded by removing such videos when flagged but struggled to proactively identify them.

- **Public Outcry**: Occasional media reports about extremist videos on YouTube led to calls for stricter oversight. People questioned whether user-driven flagging was enough, especially when certain clips could remain live long enough to garner significant views.

- **Company Response**: These issues forced YouTube to refine their terms of service, clarifying that content promoting terrorism or hate groups was explicitly banned. They also dedicated more resources to track repeated uploads of known extremist material. Though these efforts grew more robust in later years, even in 2006–2007, YouTube recognized the need for a **proactive stance**.

4.3. Privacy and Harassment

User freedom also introduced risks of **harassment** or **privacy violations**. Prank videos, hidden-camera stunts, and doxing (exposing someone's personal information) became occasional flashpoints.

- **Doxing Cases**: Occasionally, users uploaded videos revealing personal details—addresses, phone numbers—of other individuals, prompting urgent takedowns. The site's guidelines banned such behavior, but identifying malicious uploads in real time was difficult.
- **Cyberbullying**: Vicious comment threads and targeted harassment plagued some creators, especially those speaking on controversial topics. YouTube's comment system had few moderation tools beyond basic blocking, so some creators felt vulnerable to large-scale "hate raids" if they angered a particular group.

These issues highlighted the broader theme that **user-generated content** could be both a force for creativity and a conduit for harm. Though it was not illegal in the same sense as copyright infringement, these social controversies shaped YouTube's reputation and pushed the platform to refine community rules.

5. YouTube's Evolving Content Management Tools

5.1. The Beginnings of Content ID

To address **copyright concerns** more efficiently, YouTube invested in what would become **Content ID**, an automated system that scanned uploaded videos for matches to copyrighted audio or video. This technology began development in YouTube's early years, especially after repeated conflicts with music labels and film studios.

- **Matching Technology**: The system created "fingerprints" of official media, comparing new uploads to these reference files. If a match appeared, the rightsholder could choose to **block**, **track**, or **monetize** the user-uploaded version.
- **Industry Collaboration**: Building a robust fingerprint database required cooperation from large media companies, who had to supply official copies for reference. At first, some were hesitant to share, fearing leaks or unauthorized usage of their content. But as the DMCA battles grew more heated, providing reference materials began to seem like a **necessary compromise**.

Though early versions of Content ID were far from perfect, the system represented a **landmark** in user-generated content governance. It allowed rightsholders a measure of control over their works without forcing YouTube to pre-screen every video manually—an impossible task at YouTube's scale.

5.2. Community Flagging Improvements

On the **community guidelines** front, YouTube honed its flagging process to handle inappropriate or hateful content more swiftly:

1. **Flag Categories**: Users could select from multiple reasons for flagging—nudity, violence, hate speech, harassment, and so on—helping moderators route each flag to the right queue.
2. **Priority Flagging**: Certain trusted organizations or large media partners received "priority flagging" status, ensuring their complaints were addressed more quickly. This approach partly stemmed from the repeated calls by major companies to remove infringing uploads promptly.

3. **User Training**: YouTube created help articles and short tutorials guiding users on how to flag properly. They emphasized that false flagging could harm legitimate content creators, encouraging the community to only flag videos that clearly violated rules.

These improvements reflected YouTube's evolving understanding that with millions of daily uploads, community involvement was crucial for moderation. The platform's **open** nature demanded a scalable solution, blending user reports with some staff oversight.

5.3. Age Restrictions and Account Tools

In response to controversies over adult or violent videos, YouTube implemented **age gates**. If a video was flagged or deemed inappropriate for younger audiences, the system would require viewers to be logged in and confirm they were over a certain age.

- **Effectiveness**: This measure wasn't foolproof—savvy users could lie about their age. However, it signaled that YouTube was trying to keep adult content from minors without banning it outright.
- **Account Controls**: Over time, the site added more ways for creators to label their content and for viewers to **restrict** certain types of videos. Though rudimentary at first, these tools laid the groundwork for future refinement in content categorization.

Taken together, these policy updates and technical advancements showed that YouTube was **maturing** from a free-for-all upload site into a more managed environment. Yet every new measure brought questions about how much control was too much, given YouTube's emphasis on user freedom.

6. Ethical Debates: Free Speech vs. Responsibility

6.1. Balancing Openness and Regulation

One core philosophical debate centered on **free speech**. Many early YouTube users prized the platform precisely because it allowed anyone to upload a video on nearly any topic. They saw YouTube as a democratizing force in media, letting average people bypass corporate gatekeepers.

However, as disturbing, offensive, or infringing content persisted, others argued that YouTube had a **responsibility** to be more proactive. They claimed that an entirely open system could be exploited—by harassers, extremist groups, or pirates—at the expense of the common good.

YouTube's founders tried to walk a **middle path**: they wanted to keep the site as open as possible while responding to legal demands and community standards. This led to continuing tensions with critics on both sides—some who felt YouTube censored too heavily, and others who felt it did not censor enough.

6.2. International Issues and Cultural Differences

Though headquartered in the United States, YouTube quickly attracted users worldwide. This global reach intensified legal and ethical challenges:

- **Different Laws**: Some countries had stricter rules on defamation, hate speech, or political content, pressuring YouTube to remove videos that might be legal in the U.S. but **illegal elsewhere**.
- **Cultural Norms**: Content deemed harmless in one region might cause offense in another due to cultural or religious differences.
- **Localized Takedowns**: In certain cases, YouTube complied with local laws by **blocking content** in specific countries but leaving it accessible elsewhere. Critics argued this was a form of censorship; YouTube countered that it had to follow local regulations to remain operational.

These international controversies proved that a single set of global guidelines was insufficient. YouTube's early teams had to quickly learn about foreign legal frameworks and adapt policies for different markets, all while claiming to be a unified platform.

7. Impact of the Google Acquisition on Legal Strategies

7.1. Google's Resources and Legal Muscle

When Google officially **acquired YouTube** in late 2006, the site gained access to Google's vast financial and legal resources. This shifted the playing field in lawsuits and negotiations:

- **Bigger War Chest**: The potential for a massive settlement or jury award—a real threat during the Viacom case—now seemed more manageable under Google's umbrella.
- **In-House Legal Experts**: Google had a large, experienced legal team accustomed to defending the company's search engine operations under various laws. They brought expertise in intellectual property, international regulations, and privacy to YouTube's growing list of challenges.
- **Negotiating Power**: With Google behind it, YouTube had **increased leverage** in discussions with media giants. If a label or studio threatened legal action, Google's attorneys could push for licensing deals or propose collaborative solutions that smaller video sites might not have had the clout to negotiate.

For critics worried about YouTube's open platform, the acquisition introduced a new fear: that Google's involvement could lead to more intrusive data collection or heavier moderation. But from a purely **legal** perspective, having Google's backing offered a stronger shield against crippling litigation.

7.2. Shaping the Future of Content Management

Post-acquisition, YouTube accelerated development of **Content ID** and other automated tools. Google's technical expertise in machine learning and data processing guided these improvements:

- **Scale**: Where before YouTube struggled to handle tens of thousands of takedown notices, under Google they could invest in systems scanning **billions** of video uploads for potential copyright matches.
- **Advertising Integration**: Google also introduced better ad-serving technology. Over time, this made it easier for rights holders to **monetize** uploaded clips instead of demanding takedowns.
- **Policy Consistency**: By unifying certain guidelines across both Google and YouTube, the platform aimed for more consistent enforcement. This included uniform policies on hate speech or extremist content that mirrored Google's broader corporate stance.

While these developments did not solve every issue, they gave YouTube a clearer route for **long-term stability** and compliance. The era of "wild-west" uploads, with minimal oversight, gradually transformed into a more structured system—though still far more open than traditional media outlets.

8. Public Perception of YouTube's Legal Conflicts

8.1. Sympathy from Users

Many YouTube fans sympathized with the platform's plight, viewing large media corporations as **out-of-touch** or overly aggressive. The internet-savvy community championed user rights and creative remixing, believing old media companies needed to adapt to a changing landscape.

- **Comment Sections**: During high-profile disputes (like Viacom's lawsuit), users left supportive comments on YouTube's blog posts, echoing slogans about **online freedom**.
- **Grassroots Advocacy**: Some users made videos criticizing media giants or defending fair use, turning the issue into a rallying cry for digital rights. This activism, though informal, spread awareness of how crucial Safe Harbor and user freedoms were to YouTube's identity.

8.2. Concerns Over Corporate Control

On the flip side, a segment of the public worried that YouTube's decisions favored big copyright holders at the expense of individual creators. These critics felt that the **DMCA** process gave powerful companies undue influence, possibly stifling legitimate fair use or parody.

- **Fears of Censorship**: When certain takedowns seemed unjust, users accused YouTube of "selling out" or automatically siding with corporations, since failing to comply risked lawsuits.
- **Creators' Rights**: Smaller creators realized that the platform could remove their content swiftly, with few avenues for recourse beyond filing a counter-notice. This imbalance contributed to ongoing demands for more transparent dispute resolution.

Thus, YouTube walked a tightrope: it wanted to remain user-friendly and supportive of creative expression, but it also needed to avoid crippling legal battles. Striking that balance proved to be one of the platform's toughest ongoing challenges.

9. Government Scrutiny and Legislative Pressure

9.1. Calls for Stricter Regulation

Government officials, particularly in the U.S. and parts of Europe, started paying closer attention to big online platforms by 2007–2008. In some legislative circles, there were discussions about whether the DMCA itself needed updating to reflect the **new reality** of massive video-sharing sites.

- **Possible Revisions**: Some lawmakers proposed that sites like YouTube should implement **mandatory filtering** for copyrighted material, rather than relying on takedown notices.
- **Industry Lobbying**: Media companies lobbied heavily for these changes, hoping to shift the burden of copyright enforcement away from rightsholders onto the platforms

themselves. Google, on YouTube's behalf, argued that such heavy-handed measures could **stifle innovation** and hamper free expression.

9.2. International Conflicts

Beyond the U.S., various governments had their own angles:

- **European Union**: The EU considered more stringent regulations that might force platforms to pre-filter uploads. Free speech advocates warned this could lead to **over-blocking**.
- **Asia**: Some Asian countries demanded YouTube remove politically sensitive content or face bans. Though these were not purely copyright issues, they underscored how global expansions came with **varying legal standards**.

While major overhauls to the DMCA or international laws did not occur immediately, the fact that governments were debating them signaled that YouTube's legal controversies were part of a **bigger conversation** about the future of the internet.

CHAPTER 11: IMPACT ON CULTURE AND MEDIA

1. Introduction: A Shift in Entertainment Consumption

By 2006 and 2007, YouTube had evolved from a niche website for sharing home videos into a **mass phenomenon** that began reshaping the entertainment landscape. Traditional media outlets, from television networks to movie studios, watched the platform's ascent with both concern and curiosity. On the user side, people worldwide were discovering a **new way** to watch and share content. No longer bound by TV schedules or expensive production, everyday creators found an avenue for expression, and audiences discovered a nearly limitless library of clips—from comedic skits to music covers and even budding documentaries.

In this chapter, we will examine the **broader cultural and media impacts** that arose as YouTube took hold in the mid-2000s. We'll look at how it changed viewership habits, opened new doors for content creators, influenced the music industry, and drove changes in how traditional networks engaged with audiences. We will also see how YouTube's global reach allowed cultural exchange on a scale never before possible, ushering in an era where a single video could captivate viewers across the planet.

2. Democratizing Content Creation

2.1. Lowering the Barrier to Entry

Before YouTube, getting a video project seen by a large audience typically involved **pitching** it to television producers or film distributors—a process fraught with gatekeepers. With YouTube, all it took was a camera, an idea, and an internet connection. This **radical shift** empowered aspiring comedians, musicians, animators, and storytellers to bypass traditional obstacles:

1. **Affordable Equipment**
    - By the mid-2000s, consumer camcorders and even some mobile phones could record passable video. Editing software for personal computers was also becoming more accessible. This meant the cost of creating a short film, comedy sketch, or music cover was minimal compared to professional setups.
    - Creators could film content in their own homes, using free editing programs, then upload to YouTube at no cost. This simplicity invited a **wave** of experimentation, giving rise to an entire generation of internet-based creators.
2. **Direct Audience Feedback**
    - Traditional media production might take months or years, with little direct audience input until the final product aired. YouTube allowed creators to share rough videos immediately and get real-time reactions through **comments** and **ratings**.
    - This **instant feedback** loop fueled rapid improvement. Creators who saw positive responses often produced more content, refined their style, and built loyal followings in ways that TV networks could not easily replicate.
3. **Personal Branding**
    - Early YouTubers learned they could **brand** themselves with consistent intros, unique channel art, or recurring show formats. Viewers subscribed to these channels, returning for each new video. This personal approach formed intimate connections between creators and fans.
    - Unlike traditional celebrities, YouTube creators felt more **reachable**—they were not hidden behind corporate PR teams or elaborate production sets. Audiences appreciated the relatable, homemade atmosphere, spurring deeper engagement and forming small subcultures around certain channels.

By removing gatekeepers and offering direct access to an audience of millions, YouTube became a **cultural catalyst**. It opened a creative frontier where amateurs could become local or even global sensations purely on the merit of their ideas and personal charisma.

2.2. Rise of the "Prosumer"

The term **"prosumer"** refers to consumers who also produce. On YouTube, many viewers transitioned from watching others' videos to creating and uploading their own content. This phenomenon underscored a **shared identity** among users. Instead of passive spectators, they became **active participants** in shaping the platform's offerings.

1. **Cross-Pollination of Ideas**
    - A viewer might watch a comedic skit, get inspired, and post a response video. Another user would then comment, offering improvements, which the original uploader might adopt in a follow-up clip. This cycle nurtured a collective sense of ownership over the creative process.
    - As more viewers moved into content creation, YouTube's library ballooned with fresh, imaginative projects, from personal diaries to short films and how-to tutorials.

2. **Collaborative Community**
    - Groups of prosumers emerged around shared interests, such as cooking, gaming, or fashion. Within these communities, creators guest-starred on each other's channels or organized themed challenges (for instance, a "cook with me" series).
    - The ethos of prosumer culture was one of **mutual encouragement**. Success was not a zero-sum game—if one comedic channel gained attention, it could boost others by mentioning or linking them.

This **blurring of lines** between creators and consumers signaled a deep cultural change. No longer was entertainment solely produced by large studios and passively consumed by the masses. YouTube showed how an online platform could **merge** the roles of viewer and artist, with each fueling the other in a cycle of continuous creation and feedback.

3. Altering Music Discovery and Promotion

3.1. The Music Video Renaissance

Traditional music videos once aired primarily on TV channels like MTV or VH1, which curated playlists based on label deals and audience ratings. YouTube upended this system by letting artists—or fans—upload music videos directly. Suddenly, discovering music no longer hinged on cable subscriptions or a network's schedule:

1. **Access to Music from Around the World**
    - A viewer interested in a Japanese pop song or a French indie band could search on YouTube and find official or unofficial uploads in seconds. This opened global music scenes to new audiences.
    - Certain songs or artists gained **international appeal** purely through YouTube recommendations and fan shares. Listeners in South America found European metal bands; North American fans discovered K-pop idols—this cross-cultural exposure was unprecedented.
2. **Fan-Made Lyric Videos and Remixes**
    - The music community birthed creative fan-made videos, such as lyric videos or dance covers. These clips kept songs circulating and introduced them to new viewers. Although some labels worried about copyright, many recognized the **promotional value** of fans' enthusiasm.
    - Remix culture thrived as well, with amateurs re-editing music videos or combining multiple songs to create mash-ups. These fan creations, while often legally ambiguous, demonstrated how YouTube fostered a **participatory culture** in music fandom.
3. **Independent Musicians' Breakthroughs**
    - Aspiring musicians found that posting their own songs or covers could lead to discovery by record labels or direct fan support. Where a hopeful singer might once have struggled for a local gig, they now had a **global stage**.
    - Success stories began to emerge by the late 2000s, with unknown artists building huge followings on YouTube, eventually landing record deals. This signaled a **power shift**—artists no longer needed radio play or label backing to cultivate an audience.

From these changes, the music industry started recognizing YouTube as both a **promotional platform** and a potential revenue source. While the transition had its legal hiccups, there was no doubt that fans and artists alike benefited from the newfound accessibility. Viewers relished the freedom to watch and share music videos on their own terms, fueling a renaissance of interest in the visual side of music.

3.2. Talent Discovery and the Path to Fame

Another cultural hallmark was the rise of **YouTube-born stars** who could monetize their talents and gather large fan bases, sometimes turning those fan bases into successful careers offline. For instance, an unknown singer might post cover songs and watch her subscriber count soar. As fans advocated for her on social media, local news picked up the story, and eventually, a record label came calling.

1. **Cover Artists and Viral Breakouts**
   - The phenomenon of singing covers on YouTube became a gateway to stardom. Some creators meticulously produced high-quality videos—attractive lighting, strong audio, professional editing—while others used modest gear but resonated with listeners through sheer passion.
   - Viral covers of popular hits occasionally caught the eye of the original artist or their label, leading to **collaborations**, guest appearances at concerts, or even official endorsement.
2. **Connecting with Fans**
   - YouTube's comment section gave creators a **direct line** to their audience, encouraging personal connections that mainstream celebrities often lacked. Musicians thanked fans by name, asked for feedback on future uploads, and sometimes live-streamed Q&A sessions.
   - This **interactive dynamic** helped fans feel invested in a musician's journey from bedroom performances to professional stages. That emotional investment often led to consistent support—buying tracks, attending meetups, and spreading word-of-mouth publicity.
3. **Blurring Online and Offline Entertainment**
   - Some YouTube talents, once purely digital phenomena, found their way into **television** or **radio**. TV talk shows interviewed them, capitalizing on the curiosity around "internet stars."
   - The mainstream success of these once-unknown creators signified a deep cultural change: the entertainment industry began to see the online realm as a **legitimate talent incubator**, not just a hub of amateur hobbyists.

By redefining how artists reached audiences, YouTube shaped the music scene in fundamental ways. As younger viewers increasingly turned to online video for music discovery, record labels followed the crowd, forging new promotional strategies in an era where a single viral clip could propel an independent singer to instant fame.

4. Mainstream Media's Changing Relationship with YouTube

4.1. Initial Resistance and Gradual Acceptance

In YouTube's earliest period (2005–2006), major media outlets were often **skeptical** or even **hostile**. They saw user-uploaded videos of TV shows or film clips as blatant copyright infringement. However, as viral hits and rising site traffic drew public attention, some networks acknowledged YouTube's **promotional power**.

1. **Takedowns vs. Collaboration**
    - Many studios initially sent **DMCA takedown notices**, demanding the removal of any clips from their shows. Others tried to negotiate licensing deals that let them post official content while controlling advertising.
    - Over time, some networks recognized that a widely shared clip from a late-night show or a comedy sketch could boost ratings. They began **voluntarily** uploading short highlights of their programs, reaping the benefits of viral promotion.
2. **Official Channels**
    - By 2007, a growing number of TV networks and film distributors started creating **official YouTube channels**. They posted trailers, teasers, and behind-the-scenes footage, aiming to connect with the website's massive user base.
    - This shift represented a new synergy: while YouTube had once been viewed as a pirate's playground, it now became a strategic partner. Mainstream media discovered that letting fans share and comment on official uploads could broaden a show's fan base, especially among younger viewers who had drifted away from cable TV.
3. **Building a Two-Way Bridge**
    - Some talk show hosts integrated YouTube clips into their programs, highlighting funny or absurd videos found online. Audiences at home would then hop onto YouTube to search for the featured clips, reinforcing the cycle.
    - This **two-way bridge** between television and YouTube signaled a change in content distribution. TV wasn't the solitary king of visual entertainment anymore—YouTube was a new domain where networks had to adapt or risk irrelevance.

4.2. User-Generated Content on News Reports

Another notable development was how news outlets began referencing YouTube videos for **breaking stories** or human-interest pieces:

1. **Citizen Journalism**
    - Individuals at the scene of events—ranging from local accidents to political protests—could film footage on their phone and upload it to YouTube **hours** or even **minutes** later. News producers discovered and sometimes aired these raw clips, crediting the uploader or "courtesy of YouTube."
    - This approach **expanded the scope** of news coverage. Journalists could tap into a global reservoir of eyewitness videos, capturing angles or events they otherwise might miss.
2. **Viral Human-Interest Clips**
    - Stories about a lost puppy found miles away or an inventive high school robot team sometimes went viral on YouTube before traditional news outlets caught

wind. Reporters would then incorporate these viral videos into broadcast segments, effectively acknowledging that the story **originated** from an online community.
    - This phenomenon underscored how YouTube shaped the daily news cycle. The platform became a **primary source** of grassroots content, tipping off news producers to trending topics or heartfelt stories that resonated with wide audiences.
3. **Ethical and Verification Challenges**
    - Relying on user uploads came with risks: verifying authenticity was harder than with established wire services. Some newsrooms scrambled to implement **fact-checking** for internet-sourced footage.
    - Still, the overall effect was an **increased democratization** of news coverage. Viewers with phones and cameras could become quasi-reporters, bridging the gap between professional journalism and citizen observation.

These trends pointed to a future where YouTube and traditional media would become deeply intertwined. As a result, the public turned to YouTube not just for entertainment, but also for **informational content**, something that would be especially prominent during big political or social events—as explored in the next chapter about the 2008 U.S. elections.

5. Global Cultural Exchange

5.1. Breaking Down Geographic Barriers

With nearly anyone able to upload from anywhere, YouTube quickly **erased traditional borders** around media distribution. A comedic sketch filmed in Brazil could find fans in Russia; a small-town musician in the Philippines might go viral in Canada. This was a stark contrast to the era when regional TV or film distribution strictly limited international exposure.

1. **Language Differences**
    - Many early YouTube videos were not subtitled, yet their humorous or emotional content transcended language. Think of pet videos, dance routines, or physical comedy—these universal forms of entertainment drew global audiences without the need for translation.
    - As the site grew, some creators began adding **captions** or **translated subtitles**, opening their content to more viewers. Subtitling tools, though rudimentary, helped multinational fanbases form.
2. **Highlighting Cultural Traditions**
    - People uploaded festivals, cultural dances, or holiday traditions from their hometowns. Curious viewers abroad discovered these unique customs and sometimes left questions or compliments in the comments.
    - In this way, YouTube functioned as a **cross-cultural window**. It wasn't just about mainstream pop culture; the platform documented everyday life, letting viewers see beyond the typical tourist videos or scripted travel shows.
3. **Instant Dialogue Across Borders**
    - The comment sections beneath videos could become lively international forums. A user from Japan might ask about an American Thanksgiving tradition, while someone from Germany added insights into their own celebrations.

- This form of direct **people-to-people exchange** was relatively new in online video. It gave YouTube a reputation for fostering a global community, bridging differences in real time through shared media.

5.2. Amplifying Social Movements

Social activists also harnessed YouTube's global reach to spotlight issues ranging from environmental advocacy to human rights. A single protest clip could spark **global outrage** if it depicted injustice or violence:

1. **Grassroots Activism**
   - Community organizers and NGOs posted videos revealing local problems—polluted rivers, poor housing conditions, or political protests suppressed by authorities. These uploads generated sympathy or calls to action from viewers worldwide.
   - Activists recognized that a well-edited, emotionally gripping short film might gain traction via YouTube's recommendation features, pushing the cause into mainstream awareness faster than traditional methods of pamphlets or rallies.
2. **Raising Funds and Signatures**
   - Some YouTube activists linked to petitions, crowdfunding pages, or informational websites within their video descriptions. They urged viewers to **donate** or **sign** to support causes.
   - Though online donations were still a relatively novel concept in 2007, the success of certain campaigns hinted at the **power** of combining emotional video storytelling with easy online fundraising.
3. **International Solidarity**
   - When footage of a faraway conflict or disaster surfaced, sympathetic viewers from different continents left supportive comments or arranged volunteer efforts. This solidarity was not orchestrated by large institutions but rather **organically** driven by user empathy.
   - YouTube effectively became a **digital bulletin board**, bringing urgent social issues to the forefront of a global audience. This dynamic transformed how grassroots movements could mobilize, illustrating that video-sharing was far more than entertainment alone—it was also a potent tool for awareness and change.

6. The Emergence of New Advertising Models

6.1. The Beginnings of Video Advertising

Though YouTube's earliest years featured minimal ads to avoid scaring away users, the mid-2000s saw the introduction of **basic banner ads** around the site's video player. This incremental step foreshadowed a new **advertising ecosystem** in digital video:

1. **Advertisers Experiment**
   - Marketers, initially unsure about user-generated content, experimented with small campaigns on YouTube's top channels. Results varied, but some brands discovered that aligning with popular comedy or music channels yielded strong engagement.
   - The advantage for advertisers was **targeted reach**. They could place ads near videos appealing to specific demographics—teen comedy, tech reviews, or cooking channels—although targeting was still basic in 2007.
2. **Ad Integration in Official Content**

    - Mainstream media channels that posted **official** clips or series episodes started embedding short commercials to recoup costs. Fans of certain shows tolerated these ads, preferring to watch an ad-supported segment online rather than missing the content entirely.
    - This signaled a slow acceptance that YouTube's free distribution model could still incorporate **revenue streams**. Networks realized they needed to adapt, not push viewers back to TV by force.
3. **Future Monetization Hints**
    - By 2007, there were rumors of possible **revenue-sharing** models for everyday creators. The seeds of this concept were sown in discussions with Google, which had acquired YouTube. While not formally rolled out at that time, the mere hint gave amateur creators hope that they might **earn** money in the future.
    - Advertisers, meanwhile, started seeing YouTube as a distinct market from television: an interactive environment where viewers could **comment** on ads, share them, or even parody them—sparking viral brand engagement. Early comedic ads sometimes spread as widely as user-generated videos.

Although these advertising models were still in their infancy, they showed the **cultural shift** in how people perceived online content. As YouTube became an influential channel for broad audiences, brands began blending entertainment with promotions, foreshadowing the new wave of influencer marketing that would come later.

7. Criticisms and Potential Downsides

7.1. Overabundance and Quality Control

One argument critics raised was that YouTube's **open-door policy** led to a flood of low-quality videos, making it hard to separate truly creative or meaningful content from the noise. Some believed this lowered cultural standards, likening the site to a "random video dump" rather than a serious media platform.

- **Viewer Fatigue**: With so many clips, viewers sometimes struggled to discover the best material. YouTube's recommendation system was still rudimentary, so stumbling upon hidden gems took effort.
- **Curatorial Solutions**: Early in 2007, YouTube enhanced its "Featured" and "Recommended" sections to guide users toward popular or high-rated videos. This partial curation helped, but the sheer volume of uploads remained enormous.

7.2. Fragmentation of Audiences

As YouTube offered countless niche channels, critics claimed that it contributed to **audience fragmentation**. Where a unified TV audience once gathered around prime-time hits, YouTube's specialized communities allowed each viewer to follow a personal path.

- **Niche vs. Shared Experience**: This fragmentation meant fewer "watercooler moments" where everyone discussed the same show the next day. Instead, people formed smaller subcultures.
- **Upside**: On the other hand, supporters of YouTube's model saw this fragmentation as **empowerment**, letting fans of specific topics or styles connect deeply rather than being forced to watch mass-market programming.

7.3. Commercialization Concerns

Some longtime users felt uneasy watching YouTube pivot toward brand partnerships and official channels. They feared the site would lose its **authentic, grassroots ethos**, evolving into a corporate arena that overshadowed independent creators.

- **Balancing Act**: YouTube tried to reassure users that it would maintain a free, open platform. Yet the presence of more official channels introduced a tension—would user videos be pushed aside by networks with bigger budgets?
- **Growing Pains**: This was an inevitable challenge of success: as YouTube's cultural influence grew, corporate interests followed. Balancing user-generated spontaneity with the demands of large media partners became a long-term puzzle.

8. Legacy and Long-Term Influence on Media Culture

By the end of 2007, YouTube had:

- **Proven** that user-generated content could rival professional media in terms of viewership and cultural impact.

- **Popularized** a new form of celebrity, turning ordinary people with webcams into influential figures.

- **Convinced** parts of the music and TV industries that online distribution was not just a passing fad but a crucial aspect of modern entertainment.

8.1. Shifting Viewer Expectations

Viewers who grew accustomed to YouTube's **on-demand, interactive** format started to expect similar features from other media outlets. Younger demographics wanted to comment, rate, and share everything from news clips to sitcom episodes. This **interactive mindset** influenced traditional networks, pressuring them to create online portals, streaming sites, or social media presences that mirrored YouTube's immediacy.

8.2. Inspiring Future Platforms

YouTube's success inspired the launch of **countless video websites**, including those focusing on live streaming, specialized subjects, or advanced interactivity. Some were short-lived clones, while others carved out distinct niches. Regardless, YouTube's emergence acted as a **proof of concept** for investor-backed video platforms, changing the face of internet entrepreneurship.

8.3. Setting the Stage for Political and Social Impact

As we will see in the next chapter, YouTube's cultural clout extended well beyond entertainment. By 2007–2008, political campaigns recognized the potential of reaching voters directly through short, shareable video clips. Activists understood they could galvanize supporters with emotional footage of protests or critical events. The platform had moved from a novelty to a **public square** for discussion, debate, and influence.

CHAPTER 12: YOUTUBE'S ROLE IN THE 2008 U.S. ELECTIONS

1. Introduction: The Dawn of Digital Politics

In the lead-up to the **2008 U.S. presidential election**, the internet played a more significant role in politics than ever before. While political campaigns had used websites and email in previous elections, YouTube's ascendancy provided a **brand-new channel** for candidates, activists, and voters to engage with political messages. Viral videos, user-generated campaign ads, and instantaneous sharing changed the rules of election campaigning. Traditional political operatives, accustomed to TV debates and newspaper endorsements, now had to account for **online video** platforms that could instantly reach millions.

In this chapter, we will explore how YouTube became a crucial stage for the 2008 election cycle. We will see how candidates embraced the site to announce policies or address controversies, how grassroots supporters used it to spread homegrown ads, and how citizens leveraged the comments sections to debate issues in real time. This marked a turning point in political history: no longer was television the sole domain for shaping voter perception. Instead, an online community—thousands of content creators, critics, and everyday viewers—collectively influenced how campaigns unfolded.

2. Early Political Engagement on YouTube

2.1. The Rise of Campaign Channels

By 2007, major political figures recognized that YouTube offered **direct engagement** with the electorate:

1. **Official Campaign Channels**
   - Presidential hopefuls like **Barack Obama**, **Hillary Clinton**, and **John McCain** created official YouTube channels to post speeches, policy outlines, and behind-the-scenes footage. Voters no longer had to wait for TV coverage; they could subscribe and see **unfiltered** candidate updates.
   - These channels broke from the polished style of TV ads, aiming for an **informal tone** that resonated with internet-savvy voters. Candidates or their staffers might film quick backstage messages after a rally, addressing supporters directly in a personal, conversational manner.
2. **Extended Reach Without Media Gatekeepers**
   - In traditional broadcasts, networks chose which soundbites to air from a politician's event. On YouTube, campaigns uploaded **full speeches** and Q&A sessions, letting interested viewers watch the entire statement, not just a curated clip.
   - This thoroughness gave campaigns more control over their messaging and removed the editorial filters of mainstream news outlets.
3. **Subscriber Base as a Political Asset**
   - Candidates tracked channel subscriber numbers to gauge online enthusiasm. They also encouraged supporters to share links, comment, and embed campaign videos on personal blogs, turning loyal fans into **digital foot soldiers**.
   - The sense of direct connection to a candidate's feed helped foster community among supporters. People felt they were "inside" the campaign, receiving timely updates that sometimes preceded formal announcements on TV.

By leveraging YouTube, campaigns sought to build a **grassroots** movement online—raising funds, organizing local meetups, and recruiting volunteers, all with the help of readily available video content.

2.2. Early Fan-Made Ads and User Advocacy

Beyond official channels, ordinary supporters also took to YouTube to champion their preferred candidates. They created **homegrown ads**, endorsement videos, and satirical sketches—often with minimal production costs.

1. **Viral Fan Endorsements**
   - Some user-made ads gained more traction than official campaign videos. For example, a creative parody or a heartfelt personal testimonial from a relatable supporter could resonate deeply, going viral among voters.
   - Candidates who recognized the potential of these grassroots efforts sometimes **spotlighted** them in official communications, praising citizens for their initiative.

2. **Spoofs and Attack Ads**
   - Political satire flourished, with amateur comedians producing comedic "attack ads" mocking opponents or even the candidate they supported. These efforts ranged from clever or ironic jabs to crude personal attacks.
   - Voters got a sense that politics was no longer restricted to stuffy press conferences. On YouTube, it felt more like a **popular culture phenomenon**, blending humor, debate, and serious policy discourse.
3. **Group Collaborations**
   - Supporters formed groups, some official and others purely grassroots, encouraging members to upload endorsement videos under a shared hashtag. This synergy amplified the content's reach.
   - These group collaborations mimicked the "collab culture" found elsewhere on YouTube, but with a political twist: instead of comedic or musical mash-ups, users compiled endorsement or policy videos into playlists that collectively made a statement.

Through these user-driven advocacy efforts, YouTube showcased the **democratization** of political messaging. People who lacked the money to pay for TV airtime could still produce creative, attention-grabbing videos that influenced how potential voters perceived a candidate or an issue.

3. Influencing Public Opinion Through User-Generated Content

3.1. Reaction Videos to Debates and Speeches

One immediate outcome of YouTube's engagement with politics was the rise of **reaction videos** to high-profile campaign events:

1. **Debate Highlights**
   - When televised debates aired, viewers quickly clipped key moments and uploaded them to YouTube—often within hours or even minutes of the live broadcast ending.
   - Reaction videos showed everyday people filming themselves responding to a candidate's words. They might praise a policy stance, call out perceived errors, or fact-check statements. These personal insights offered a **ground-level** view of public sentiment.
2. **Instant Analysis**
   - Political pundits and bloggers embedded YouTube debate clips in their write-ups, providing timestamps to show exactly where a candidate stumbled or delivered a memorable line.
   - This synergy between mainstream commentary and user-uploaded highlights meant debates reached a broader audience—particularly young voters who didn't watch traditional TV. They could skip the entire broadcast, focusing instead on YouTube's curated "must-see" moments.
3. **Community Discussions**
   - The comment sections under debate clips often became a microcosm of the broader political dialogue—partisan bickering, thoughtful analysis, and comedic jabs all mingled in the same threads.
   - Though messy and sometimes vitriolic, these online discussions **activated** people who might not have engaged with politics through formal channels. Even heated

arguments signaled that more citizens were paying attention to campaign messages and forming opinions.

Through reaction videos and community discussions, YouTube functioned as an **informal town hall**, bringing together supporters and opponents in direct conversation. This heightened the sense that politics was no longer confined to newsrooms or private fundraisers—it was something everyday people could actively shape.

3.2. Fact-Checking and Candidate Accountability

Another hallmark of YouTube's political influence was how easy it became for users, journalists, or rival campaigns to **fact-check** politicians:

1. **Documenting Contradictions**
    - A candidate might make a statement in one speech and a seemingly opposite statement in another. Users compiled these conflicting clips into **"gotcha" videos**, challenging the candidate's credibility.
    - In an earlier era, journalists had to rely on transcripts or older broadcast tapes. YouTube allowed direct side-by-side video comparisons, making the evidence instantly **visual** and shareable.
2. **Citizen Fact-Checkers**
    - Ordinary viewers used YouTube to highlight questionable claims by politicians. They might overlay text citations on top of a candidate's speech, referencing data from official sources to refute or confirm the politician's statements.
    - This approach gave the average person a sense of **empowerment**—they weren't simply absorbing campaign rhetoric; they were actively verifying or disproving it in front of a wide online audience.
3. **Candidate Accountability**
    - Knowing that any snippet of a speech could be uploaded and dissected on YouTube forced campaigns to tread more carefully. A controversial remark in a local town hall no longer remained local—it could go viral overnight.
    - While some politicians resented this intense scrutiny, many adapted, refining their messaging to reduce the chance of damaging viral moments.

YouTube thus played a **watchdog role**, shifting some power from media gatekeepers to everyday users who used the platform to hold leaders accountable. This mirrored broader trends in digital journalism but was particularly impactful in the heated atmosphere of a presidential election.

4. YouTube's Sponsored Debates and Partnerships

4.1. YouTube and CNN Debates

One of the most notable collaborations of the 2008 election was the **CNN-YouTube Debates**. These events illustrated how a mainstream news network and a cutting-edge online platform could join forces:

1. **User-Submitted Questions**

- Instead of traditional debate moderators formulating all questions, CNN invited Americans to **record video questions** and submit them via YouTube. Then, CNN selected some to be played on air during the live debate.
- This concept gave everyday voters a direct voice, forcing candidates to address the concerns of a single mother in Iowa or a student in California—people who wouldn't usually have a platform in major televised debates.

2. **Videos of All Selected Questions**
    - CNN posted the chosen questions on its own website and on YouTube before and after the debates, allowing broader public discussion. Supporters or critics could examine the queries, praising or complaining about CNN's choices.
    - This **transparency** was a departure from typical debate processes, where questions came from professional journalists. The partnership with YouTube lent a feeling of **inclusive populism** to the debates.
3. **Impact on Viewership**
    - Ratings for these debates were higher than expected, partly due to the **novelty** of YouTube's involvement. Younger audiences, historically less engaged in politics, tuned in out of curiosity about how user videos would shape the discussion.
    - The debates also generated **massive post-event traffic** on YouTube, as people looked up clips of candidates' responses or shared their own reaction videos.

Through such partnerships, YouTube showed it could **bridge** traditional broadcast formats with user interactivity. The CNN-YouTube debates became a landmark moment, symbolizing how the internet was no longer just an echo chamber for political junkies—it was central to campaign discourse.

4.2. Co-Sponsored Town Halls

Beyond high-profile debates, YouTube experimented with smaller, **town hall-style** forums, sometimes co-sponsoring with local media or political organizations:

1. **Live Streams with Chat**
    - Some events streamed live on YouTube, allowing viewers to submit questions in a chat window. Although chat moderation was basic, it gave real-time feedback to politicians on stage.
    - Campaigns recognized these digital events could reach **diaspora communities** or far-flung supporters who couldn't attend in person.
2. **Focus on Youth Voting**
    - Many of these co-sponsored forums targeted **young voters**, encouraging college students to speak directly to candidates about issues like tuition costs or job prospects. YouTube provided an accessible medium for them to voice concerns.
    - This approach sought to reverse historically low youth turnout, hoping interactive video sessions might **motivate** more first-time voters.
3. **Local Political Races**
    - While presidential campaigns got the most attention, smaller races—like congressional or gubernatorial campaigns—also used YouTube to hold digital forums. This brought local politics into the same space, leveling the playing field for lesser-known candidates.

- Voters could watch archived streams of these forums anytime, not limited by a broadcast schedule, making it easier to do research on local candidates' platforms.

These collaborative events further integrated YouTube into the fabric of political campaigning. Rather than an outsider tool, it became a **recognized partner** in fostering public debate. The result was a sense that the 2008 election wasn't just about stump speeches and televised rallies but about **two-way communication** between politicians and a more empowered, tech-savvy electorate.

5. Grassroots Fundraising and Campaign Organization

5.1. Linking Video to Donation Platforms

Although YouTube itself wasn't a fundraising platform, campaigns soon discovered that a compelling video could steer viewers to **donation pages**. In 2007–2008:

1. **Video Appeals**
   - A candidate might upload a short, heartfelt message urging supporters to donate $5 or $10. By inserting links in the video description, campaigns made it easy for viewers to **click through** to official fundraising sites.
   - Some smaller campaigns used personalized video "shout-outs," thanking individual donors or mention them in the next video if they contributed a certain amount—blending social media's personalization with fundraising efforts.
2. **User-Led Donation Drives**
   - Supporters often launched their own micro-campaigns on YouTube, challenging fellow users to donate to a candidate within a set timeframe. They'd post proof of their donation, encouraging others to do the same.
   - This **peer-driven approach** harnessed group psychology—if a user saw multiple "I donated!" videos from peers, they might feel compelled to join in.
3. **Trackable Impact**
   - Campaigns could measure a spike in donations after releasing a particularly effective or emotional video. This data-driven approach helped them refine their messages: emotional appeals, comedic relief, or policy clarifications that resonated best with viewers.
   - The clarity of these analytics gave campaigns a sense of **direct ROI** on their video content, fostering more creative experiments.

By bridging emotive storytelling with immediate donation links, YouTube provided a **seamless funnel** from inspiration to financial support. This mechanism proved especially valuable to candidates who relied on many small contributions rather than a few large donors.

5.2. Organization of Volunteer Networks

Campaign supporters also capitalized on YouTube to **coordinate events** and share updates on volunteer work:

1. **Vlogging Volunteer Experiences**

- People posted video diaries of canvassing neighborhoods, phone-banking sessions, or setting up campaign rallies. This personal perspective **humanized** the campaign process, making it seem accessible and even fun.
- Others used these vlogs to recruit more volunteers, providing tips and advice on how to approach potential voters or handle policy questions.

2. **Instructional Videos**
    - Campaign staffers and grassroots groups alike uploaded tutorials on tasks like voter registration procedures or how to host a local campaign meetup.
    - These how-to clips democratized campaign operations—anyone with internet access could learn best practices, from distributing flyers to setting up a local debate watch party.
3. **Sense of Community and Motivation**
    - As volunteers saw each other's videos, they built a **virtual community**. A new volunteer in Florida might feel a kinship with seasoned canvassers in Ohio, simply by watching their supportive messages on YouTube.
    - Sharing these experiences boosted morale, especially for underdog campaigns that relied heavily on volunteer enthusiasm rather than big-budget advertising.

Hence, YouTube transcended the role of a mere broadcasting channel. It operated as a **logistical hub** for political organizing—teaching, motivating, and connecting local volunteers into a cohesive movement that spanned states or even the entire country.

6. Controversies and Criticisms in the Political Arena

6.1. Negative Ads and Misinformation

While YouTube enabled positive grassroots engagement, it also opened the door to **negative campaigning** and misinformation:

1. **Attack Videos**
    - Detractors of any candidate could upload harshly edited "attack ads," sometimes twisting facts or presenting out-of-context statements to smear reputations. The anonymity of user accounts made it easy for unscrupulous groups to flood the platform with deceptive material.
    - These videos often spread quickly, especially if they triggered strong emotional reactions among partisans.
2. **Fake Endorsements and Satire Confusion**
    - Some videos impersonated official campaigns or political figures, confusing viewers about whether a piece of content was **real** or **satirical**. This led to calls for better authentication.
    - YouTube responded by allowing political campaigns to **verify** official channels, but user-generated spoofs continued. The blurred line between comedic parody and malicious misinformation persisted as a point of tension.
3. **Limited Fact-Checking Tools**
    - Although many users attempted to fact-check, the platform itself offered no robust system for labeling verified or debunked content. Political misinformation thus slipped through, shaping opinions before credible sources could respond.

Critics warned that YouTube's **low barrier** to uploading videos made it a prime vehicle for propaganda. While the platform expanded free speech, it also raised questions about how to balance that freedom with the dangers of misleading or harmful political content.

6.2. Personal Attacks and Online Harassment

Beyond official attacks, some candidates or their families found themselves targeted by **online harassment**, fueled by the ease of posting hateful comments or personal rumors:

1. **Comment Section Toxicity**
    - The same comment system that allowed lively debate also fostered hateful remarks and slurs. Some candidates' official YouTube videos were flooded with personal attacks rather than policy discussions.
    - Campaign staff sometimes disabled comments on official channels to block harassment—drawing criticism for suppressing user feedback.
2. **Privacy Breaches**
    - In extreme cases, users leaked personal data or made threats. These incidents highlighted the darker side of online engagement, where anonymity emboldened trolls or political extremists.
    - YouTube's moderation tools were still fairly limited, forcing campaigns to invest additional resources in policing offensive content or spamming.
3. **Candidate Reactions**
    - Some politicians addressed online hate directly, filming a short YouTube clip to acknowledge or condemn attacks. Others preferred to **ignore** the hostility, focusing on official messages. Each approach revealed how campaigns navigated the **unfiltered** nature of the internet.

While these issues did not overshadow the broad positives of digital campaigning, they underscored the complexity of letting anyone post freely in a heated election cycle.

7. Outcome and Lasting Influence on Political Campaigns

7.1. Effect on Voter Engagement

By Election Day 2008, it was clear that **millions** of voters—especially younger ones—had used YouTube as part of their political experience. While precise data on direct influence is challenging to measure, the general sentiment was that **online political videos** drove unprecedented engagement among demographics once considered politically apathetic.

- **Higher Youth Turnout**: Analysts credited increased youth turnout, in part, to social media activism and the sense of **community** found online. YouTube's role in delivering direct, relatable content played a significant role in galvanizing younger voters.

- **Policy Awareness**: Even outside the youth bracket, many voters felt more informed after watching unfiltered speeches or user-generated breakdowns of policies, bypassing mainstream media's editorial framing.

7.2. Campaign Strategies Permanently Altered

The 2008 election solidified YouTube as an **essential** political tool:

1. **Ongoing Channel Maintenance**
    - Post-election, winning and losing candidates alike kept official channels active to maintain contact with constituents. Even local officials realized the power of YouTube for **public announcements** or feedback sessions.
    - This continuous presence indicated that short, direct videos were no longer a campaign gimmick—they were part of modern political communication.
2. **Future Campaign Blueprints**
    - Strategies tested in 2008—such as user-generated content drives, rapid response videos, and real-time fact-checking—became **standard practice** in subsequent campaigns.
    - Parties hired dedicated digital teams to handle YouTube uploads, moderate comments, and plan viral marketing stunts. The new era of "campaign 2.0" demanded proficiency in online video outreach.

7.3. Setting Expectations for Political Transparency

YouTube's role in 2008 also raised public expectations: voters grew accustomed to **seeing** their politicians in unscripted settings, answering questions directly to a camera. Politicians who avoided or dismissed these online platforms risked appearing out of touch.

- **Pressure for Consistency**: Because old clips could resurface at any time, candidates learned to keep their messages consistent across states and events, or risk being called out online.

- **Civic Engagement**: Some hopeful observers believed this shift could foster a **more informed** electorate, while skeptics warned about echo chambers and misinformation. Yet few denied that YouTube had **reshaped** how political dialogue took place.

CHAPTER 13: INTERNATIONAL EXPANSION

1. Introduction: The Global Appetite for Online Video

By late 2007 and early 2008, YouTube was widely recognized as one of the internet's fastest-growing platforms. Originally launched in the United States, the site's influence had quickly crossed borders. Users from all over the world were uploading content in various languages—even before YouTube offered any localized site versions. As broadband internet spread and camera phones became more common, more regions demanded an easy way to share and watch videos. Recognizing this trend, YouTube's team decided to accelerate the creation of localized versions of the site, complete with translations and region-specific features.

This chapter delves into YouTube's **international expansion** efforts during its early years. We will see why the company considered a global strategy crucial, how it adapted to local laws and cultural norms, and the unique challenges it faced while rolling out language-specific websites. We will also explore how foreign markets responded to YouTube's arrival, the role of government regulations, and how localized YouTube communities shaped the platform's worldwide identity.

2. The Motivations Behind Going Global

2.1. Meeting Worldwide User Demand

From its earliest days, YouTube was never limited to American audiences. People from across Europe, Asia, Latin America, and Africa stumbled upon the site, drawn by its user-generated content and easy-to-use interface. Even if the site was primarily in English, many found they could still navigate well enough to watch, upload, and share videos.

1. **User Curiosity**
    - Content in one language often attracted viewers who did not speak that language but enjoyed the visuals or music. For example, comedic sketches, dance routines, or short documentaries transcended linguistic barriers.
    - Some users posted translations or subtitles, or created text overlays to explain the gist of a video, helping break down language walls in a grassroots manner.
2. **Daily Interaction**
    - International visitors still wanted YouTube to feel more accessible—providing menu items, help pages, and instructions in their native languages. They also wanted localized categories to highlight local news, pop culture, and trending videos relevant to their region.
3. **Increasing Broadband Adoption**
    - As more countries expanded broadband internet access, entire populations of new users came online, primed to share personal videos. The demand for a platform like YouTube rose steadily, prompting the company to seize the opportunity before competitors established a foothold abroad.

2.2. Business and Competitive Pressures

Beyond user demand, YouTube's **business strategy** also pushed it toward localization:

1. **Staving Off Local Rivals**
    - In some countries, local video-sharing sites had a strong presence. For instance, Dailymotion in France, Tudou and Youku in China, and other regional platforms catered to specific linguistic audiences. YouTube did not want to lose potential users to these localized offerings.
    - By customizing the YouTube interface and content recommendations for different languages or regions, the company aimed to be the **first choice** in every market.
2. **Advertising and Revenue**
    - Advertisers in various countries were more willing to invest if YouTube offered local ad systems, local user data, and the ability to target region-specific audiences.
    - Establishing local partnerships and brand deals required a presence "on the ground," not just a translated interface. YouTube saw the financial potential in broadening its user base beyond English-speaking nations.
3. **Google's International Reach**
    - Since Google acquired YouTube in late 2006, the platform could tap into Google's vast global infrastructure—data centers, local business teams, and established

relationships with advertisers worldwide. This synergy made the jump to multiple countries more feasible.

- Google's own international expansion offered a template: localizing the search experience country by country. YouTube's leadership saw a chance to replicate that success with video-sharing.

3. The Rollout of Localized YouTube Sites

3.1. The First Wave of Localized Versions

In 2007, YouTube began launching **country-specific portals**. For example, "YouTube UK" (United Kingdom) came with localized homepage features, showing British news, regional trending videos, and local channels. Similar portals appeared for Canada, Brazil, France, Ireland, Italy, Japan, the Netherlands, Poland, Spain, and other countries.

1. **Language Translations**
   - The user interface—menu links, category names, and instructions—was translated into local languages where English was not dominant. This allowed users to navigate the site more comfortably.
   - YouTube also tried to **localize** the way content was displayed, for instance grouping local trending videos or recommending region-specific creators at the top of each user's feed.
2. **Local Domain Extensions**
   - Each localized version often had a domain extension like .co.uk or .fr. This signaled to users that the site was tailored for their country, though the overall brand remained "YouTube."
   - Some users manually switched to foreign versions just to see what was popular elsewhere, adding a cultural exchange aspect even among localized sites.
3. **Cultural Adaptations**
   - For the homepage, YouTube curated content featuring local celebrities, comedic styles, or music trends. This approach helped new users feel the platform had content relevant to their daily life and entertainment scene.
   - In some regions, local teams worked with popular vloggers or influencers to promote the new site version, kicking off promotional events or contests that encouraged users to explore the localized platform.

3.2. Challenges in Translation and Adaptation

Going global was not as simple as flipping a language switch:

1. **Dialects and Language Variants**
   - In countries with multiple regional languages—like India or Spain—YouTube had to decide whether to support them all at once or start with the most widely spoken. This sometimes stirred debate among local users who felt underrepresented if their dialect was left out.
   - Even within a single language, differences in slang or spelling (e.g., British vs. American English) required careful attention to ensure the platform felt "authentic" to local users.
2. **Local Infrastructure**

    - Some regions had slower average internet speeds or less reliable connections. YouTube needed to ensure videos buffered quickly. The platform set up local caching servers or partnered with internet providers to handle data traffic more efficiently.
    - Countries with heavy internet censorship or strict data regulations posed additional hurdles. For instance, in markets like China, YouTube's content policies clashed with government restrictions, complicating or even preventing an official launch.
3. **Support and Moderation**
    - As localized user bases grew, so did the **moderation workload**. YouTube had to hire or train support staff who spoke local languages, capable of handling DMCA claims, community guideline enforcement, and user questions in those regions.
    - Cultural standards differed: certain jokes or scenes considered acceptable in one country might be offensive in another. YouTube had to refine guidelines to account for local norms without fragmenting its global policy too severely.

Despite these complexities, the introduction of local sites generally sparked an **uptick in user engagement**. Many new creators emerged, comfortable expressing themselves in their native tongue. Meanwhile, advertisers found local campaigns more attractive, bringing in revenue that helped offset the platform's high operational costs.

4. Cultural Acceptance and Challenges

4.1. Enthusiastic Reception in Some Regions

In many countries, YouTube's arrival was met with excitement:

1. **Instant Popularity in Brazil**
    - Brazil had a large youth demographic active on social media. When YouTube launched a Portuguese interface and a .br domain, Brazilians quickly embraced it for comedy sketches, football (soccer) highlights, and personal vlogs. Brazilian YouTubers began amassing large followings, reflecting the country's vibrant online culture.
    - Partnerships with local TV shows and pop stars further boosted awareness.
2. **Rapid Growth in Japan**
    - Japan's robust broadband infrastructure supported high-quality uploads. Early localized features let Japanese users share everything from anime fan tributes to daily life vlogs in crowded cityscapes.
    - The local YouTube team collaborated with Japanese media companies to post official music videos and TV show clips, offsetting some copyright concerns. This approach helped legitimize YouTube as more than just an amateur video site.
3. **Expanding in Europe**
    - Countries like France, Spain, and Germany saw strong uptake, with new local music and comedic content catering to national tastes. Many YouTubers in these countries had English-speaking international audiences as well, forming bilingual or subtitled channels that bridged cultural gaps.

4.2. Resistance or Regulatory Hurdles Elsewhere

Not all markets welcomed YouTube with open arms:

1. **China's Stringent Internet Rules**
    - The "Great Firewall" in China blocked or restricted many foreign sites. YouTube occasionally faced **complete blocks** after certain politically sensitive videos circulated. Attempts to launch a fully localized Chinese version stalled, as the platform could not comply with the government's censorship demands without compromising its community standards.
    - Domestic Chinese rivals (Youku, Tudou) thrived under these circumstances, limiting YouTube's official presence.
2. **Government Concerns in Middle Eastern Countries**
    - In some Middle Eastern nations, authorities restricted content deemed culturally or politically sensitive. When user-uploaded videos criticized leaders or covered taboo subjects, governments pressured YouTube to remove them or face potential blocks.
    - YouTube tried negotiating limited region-locking of specific videos—making them inaccessible in certain countries—rather than global takedowns. Still, repeated controversies led to tensions and occasional site blackouts.
3. **Patchwork of European Copyright Laws**
    - Even within Europe, each country had distinct copyright regulations and collecting societies for music. YouTube had to negotiate separate licensing agreements, a tedious and expensive task. Disputes sometimes led to certain music videos or channel features being blocked in specific European markets.

Despite these setbacks, YouTube continued to see net global growth. Countries that allowed relatively open access often became robust communities. Where the platform faced censorship or legal complications, user interest still existed, but official expansions were throttled or forced into compromise.

5. Partnerships with Foreign Media and Creators

5.1. Collaboration with International Broadcasters

To gain credibility and defuse tensions, YouTube pursued **partnerships** with TV networks, production houses, and music labels worldwide:

1. **Licensing Deals**
    - In markets like the UK or Japan, signing deals with major broadcasters allowed them to upload highlights or even full episodes. This mix of professional content gave local audiences a reason to visit YouTube regularly.
    - Revenue-sharing models were hammered out case by case, especially regarding advertising. Some broadcasters preferred promotional benefits (exposure for their shows), while others wanted direct ad income from views.
2. **Dedicated Channels**
    - The BBC in the UK, for example, created official channels showcasing clips from popular programs like Top Gear or Doctor Who. Japanese TV stations posted variety show highlights. Some Latin American networks offered telenovela recaps.

    - These official channels lent a sense of **legitimacy** to the local YouTube site and eased fears that the platform was just a haven for pirated re-uploads.
3. **Cross-Promotion**
    - YouTube's local teams co-hosted events with broadcasters or ran official "YouTube Nights" on certain shows, featuring top viral clips from the region. This cross-promotion encouraged TV viewers to check out full versions or behind-the-scenes footage online.
    - By bridging TV and online video, both sides benefited: networks tapped into younger digital audiences, while YouTube gained mainstream acceptance.

5.2. Spotlighting International YouTube Stars

Local creators often needed a boost to reach audiences, especially in markets where the idea of a "YouTube star" was new:

1. **Featured Sections and Contests**
    - YouTube's homepage in each country often displayed "Featured Creators," "Rising Stars," or "Local Spotlight" areas. These features guided users to emerging vloggers, comedians, or musicians in their own language.
    - Competitions like "Japan's Next Vlogger" or "La Nueva Estrella de YouTube" (The New YouTube Star) in Spanish-speaking countries offered cash prizes or front-page exposure. This built excitement around content creation as a legitimate pursuit.
2. **Music Partnerships**
    - For local indie musicians, YouTube sometimes organized contests or collaborated with music festivals, inviting fans to vote online. Winners performed live at events or received professional studio time.
    - These initiatives established YouTube as a channel for local cultural expression, not just imported American memes or Hollywood trailers

3. **Influencer Gatherings**
   - Early gatherings or informal "meetups" also happened abroad. YouTube staff would host sessions where local creators shared tips and best practices. These gatherings built creative communities, forging relationships among YouTubers who later cross-promoted each other's channels.
   - The platform also occasionally ran workshops on monetization or content policy, underscoring that YouTube wanted creators to thrive.

By highlighting local talent, YouTube nurtured each region's sense of ownership over the site, ensuring it wasn't perceived as merely an American import. This approach turned localized YouTube sites into active cultural arenas, reflecting each country's humor, music, and social issues.

6. Content Localization and Policy Adjustments

6.1. Dealing with Language-Specific Content

While comedic sketches or music videos translate well visually, some content is heavily tied to language, such as monologues, educational channels, or local political commentary. YouTube adapted by:

1. **Subtitle and Caption Tools**
   - The platform introduced basic closed-captioning features, letting creators provide translations. While not perfect, these tools helped popular channels expand their audiences beyond one language group.
   - Automated captioning was in its infancy, often struggling with accuracy. Still, the feature signaled YouTube's commitment to bridging language gaps.
2. **Local Tagging and Categories**
   - YouTube encouraged creators to use language-specific tags and video descriptions. By analyzing these tags, the recommendation algorithm could better suggest relevant videos to viewers in that region.
   - Country-based trending pages highlighted top videos in local languages rather than burying them under global hits.
3. **Channel Language Settings**
   - Creators could set their channel's primary language, enabling the interface to display relevant ads and recommended videos. This step streamlined how local advertisers targeted audiences.

6.2. Community Guidelines and Regional Sensitivities

As YouTube expanded internationally, it encountered different norms about nudity, violence, religion, and political speech:

1. **Varying Cultural Norms**
   - In some conservative societies, content with mild nudity might be considered more offensive than it would be in more liberal regions. Similarly, comedic sketches mocking certain religious figures could provoke backlash.

    - YouTube tried to maintain **one set** of community guidelines while respecting local laws. This led to "geoblocking" certain videos in countries where they might be illegal or widely offensive, while remaining accessible elsewhere.
2. **Handling Hate Speech and Ethnic Tensions**
    - Some countries had laws prohibiting expressions of hate or denial of historical atrocities (e.g., Holocaust denial in parts of Europe). YouTube faced demands to remove such content or risk legal consequences.
    - The platform partnered with local advocacy groups in certain regions, refining how it identified and flagged hateful uploads. These relationships helped interpret the nuances of local conflict zones or interethnic hostilities.
3. **Transparency vs. Censorship**
    - Critics accused YouTube of bowing to government censorship in certain markets. Each time a government demanded the removal of political dissent videos, the platform faced a dilemma—comply or be shut down entirely in that country.
    - Internally, the company weighed whether partial service was better than no service at all. Each decision sparked debates about user rights, freedom of expression, and business interests. Over time, these controversies shaped YouTube's reputation as both an open platform and a company willing to compromise under legal pressure.

While not every international expansion was smooth, the overall result was that YouTube **tailored** itself to fit a wide range of cultural landscapes. By the end of 2008, localized versions covered a significant portion of the globe, connecting creators and viewers in myriad languages.

7. The Emergence of Global Influencers

7.1. Cross-Border Collaboration

As localized sites took root, creators from different countries began to **collaborate**:

1. **Joint Projects**
    - A French comedy channel might team up with a Brazilian gaming vlogger to produce a short comedic sketch, each speaking their own language but adding subtitles. The novelty of cross-cultural teamwork intrigued audiences, expanding both creators' fan bases internationally.
    - Music collabs were also popular. Singers or bands from different continents recorded duets or mash-ups. Their respective viewers discovered new genres or languages, fueling a sense of global connection.
2. **Global Challenges**
    - Viral challenges—like dance trends or comedic skits—spread across local YouTube communities, eventually exploding into worldwide phenomena. Each region's creators added their cultural twist or language flair, then shared back to the global audience.
    - This interplay of local adaptation and global sharing turned YouTube into a **melting pot** of cultural exchange, fueling a sense that the platform was truly universal.

7.2. Rising Transnational Fanbases

Certain creators transcended language barriers, finding fans in multiple countries:

1. **Nonverbal or Musical Content**
    - Channels focusing on physical comedy, magic tricks, cooking demonstrations, or purely instrumental music were easier to appreciate without a shared language. These creators often racked up views from dozens of countries, generating comment sections brimming with different languages.
    - Some savvy YouTubers learned to greet viewers in multiple languages, recognizing the broad reach of their audience.
2. **Bilingual or Multilingual Channels**
    - Creators who spoke multiple languages might record separate versions of each video or offer bilingual commentary, doubling their potential audience. This demanded extra effort but could yield substantial growth internationally.
    - Such channels represented a unique shift: previously, popular content was almost always anchored in one language. Now, the platform embraced polyglot formats as part of its identity.
3. **Fan Subtitling**
    - In some cases, dedicated fans voluntarily translated their favorite creator's videos into various languages, uploading subtitle files. These crowd-sourced translations let channels break through linguistic walls even if creators themselves spoke only one language.
    - This spirit of volunteer collaboration highlighted how YouTube's global community could support creators they loved, contributing labor to expand a channel's appeal.

The rise of global influencers showed that YouTube was not just exporting American or English-language content—it was **importing** new voices from everywhere, forging an interconnected web of online personalities. These developments hinted at how, in the long run, the platform would foster a worldwide content creator ecosystem far more diverse than any single region's media industry.

8. Growing Pains: Moderation, Monetization, and Censorship Abroad

8.1. Moderation Overload

Expanding globally brought a surge in uploads:

1. **Spikes in Copyright Claims**
    - As each new country introduced local entertainment content—music, TV, movies—the volume of potential copyright infringements grew. YouTube's legal and moderation teams had to handle more takedown notices from numerous collecting societies and rights holders.
    - While Content ID (in its early versions) helped automate identification, it was far from comprehensive. The burden of manual reviews and user disputes rose steeply.
2. **Cultural Offenses and Hate Speech**
    - With more users from diverse backgrounds, hateful or abusive content also increased. What one group found comedic could be deeply insulting to another.

Some videos spurred local protests, adding pressure for faster removal or censorship.
    - The language barrier complicated moderation. The site needed staff or volunteers fluent in regional languages to confirm the context of flagged content. Automated detection of sensitive keywords often misfired due to slang or subtext.
3. **Corporate Resource Strain**
    - Although Google's backing helped, the sheer scale of global expansion put constant strain on YouTube's servers, support staff, and policy teams. The speed of growth sometimes outpaced the platform's ability to respond effectively to local controversies.

8.2. Local Ad Models and Monetization

By 2008, YouTube was testing ways to serve region-specific ads, hoping to **monetize** foreign markets:

1. **Localization for Advertisers**
    - Large companies in Europe or Asia wanted to run local-language video ads. YouTube adapted its ad systems to handle multiple currencies, billing practices, and data rules (especially in the EU).
    - This move made local ad campaigns more appealing, increasing revenue potential. Yet each country's regulations around advertising—especially for products like alcohol, pharmaceuticals, or certain political ads—required careful compliance.
2. **Creator Monetization**
    - At this stage, official monetization for creators outside the U.S. was limited or nonexistent. YouTube was cautious about rolling out ad-sharing globally, partly due to legal complexities and the challenge of setting up payment systems in multiple currencies.
    - Some local creators felt overlooked, seeing YouTubers in the U.S. begin to earn ad revenue while they had no such option. Tensions arose in certain communities, pushing YouTube to promise that broader creator monetization would eventually expand internationally.
3. **Brand Partnerships**
    - Outside of direct ad revenue, some successful foreign YouTubers struck deals with local brands, placing product placements or sponsor shoutouts in their videos. The platform was not always directly involved, but this phenomenon hinted at future "influencer marketing" trends.
    - YouTube sometimes hosted seminars or guides teaching creators how to handle sponsorships ethically, ensuring disclaimers or transparency about paid promotions, though policies were still evolving.

8.3. Government Pressures to Remove Content

In addition to censorship requests, certain countries threatened to **shut down** YouTube if demands were not met:

1. **Political Dissent Videos**
    - In some regions, videos criticizing the ruling government or exposing corruption gained traction. Authorities demanded YouTube remove them. If YouTube refused, access to the entire site risked being blocked.
    - The platform often negotiated partial compliance—blocking specific videos only for IP addresses in that country—while keeping them accessible globally.
2. **Religious Sensitivities**
    - Instances of perceived blasphemy or disrespect to religious figures sparked large-scale protests in certain countries. Governments blamed YouTube for hosting the content. The site faced repeated toggles of block/unblock statuses.
    - These episodes ignited debates about local respect vs. global free speech. YouTube's stance varied case by case, balancing local laws with the platform's open ethos.
3. **Transparency Reports**
    - In later years, YouTube (and Google) began publishing basic data on government takedown requests, though the specifics of each request often remained confidential. Even in these early days, internal records showed a growing wave of official demands from around the globe.

Despite these political entanglements, user demand in many countries remained high, proving that YouTube served a fundamental desire for **self-expression** and access to unfiltered content. Each new localized rollout typically boosted daily traffic, making the platform an increasingly vital part of international digital culture.

CHAPTER 14: EVOLVING TECHNOLOGY AND FEATURES

1. Introduction: The Need for Technological Innovation

From 2005 through 2008, YouTube's user base skyrocketed. More uploads, more viewers, and more global presence meant the site needed robust **technical solutions** to deliver a reliable, fast experience. In its earliest incarnation, YouTube's simple interface and Flash-based playback served millions of basic, low-resolution clips. But as cameras improved, broadband speeds rose, and user expectations grew, YouTube had to **upgrade** behind the scenes and at the user interface level.

This chapter delves into how YouTube **evolved its technology and features** in the mid-to-late 2000s—improving video quality, transitioning from Flash to alternative formats, optimizing mobile experiences, and introducing tools that made content discovery and engagement easier. We will also examine how new features, such as HD playback or advanced analytics, shaped the user and creator experience. These changes were key to YouTube's continued success, preventing it from becoming outdated or overshadowed by new competitors.

2. The Transition from Flash to Improving Video Formats

2.1. Early Reliance on Flash Playback

When YouTube first launched, **Macromedia (later Adobe) Flash** was the dominant technology for embedded web videos. Users could watch clips in any browser that had the Flash plugin, which many did by default. This standardization was a major **selling point**, as it bypassed the messy compatibility issues of older media players like RealPlayer or Windows Media.

1. **Advantages of Flash**
    - Flash allowed inline video playback, meaning viewers did not have to open a separate application. This convenience was a key factor in YouTube's early user-friendliness.
    - The site encoded all uploads into a single Flash Video format (.flv), reducing the complexity of supporting multiple codecs. This simplified engineering tasks but placed constraints on video quality.
2. **Limitations**
    - As hardware and internet speeds improved, Flash's performance began to show **weaknesses**—especially in high-resolution playback.
    - Flash also required frequent plugin updates. Users with outdated versions often faced playback issues or security flaws, leading to a subpar experience in certain cases.

2.2. Experimenting with Higher Quality and H.264

Around 2007, as viewers demanded sharper images and better audio, YouTube started **experimenting** with new encoding formats:

1. **H.264 Introduction**
    - The H.264 codec offered higher quality at relatively lower bitrates, making it ideal for streaming more detailed content without overwhelming user bandwidth. YouTube began transcoding some videos to H.264 for an "HQ" or "High Quality" option.
    - Early tests showed improved clarity, especially in videos with lots of motion or text overlays.
2. **User Reactions**
    - Many viewers were excited about the improved clarity. However, not all devices or browsers supported H.264 playback in the same way. For compatibility, YouTube still offered a fallback Flash-based stream.
    - Creators quickly realized that uploading a higher resolution source video could yield a crisper final product, so they began filming in 480p or 720p if possible—still modest by modern standards but a leap forward from the older 240p or 360p norms.
3. **Challenges in Rolling Out**
    - Upgrading the entire library to new codecs was a massive job. YouTube had to re-encode millions of existing videos. This demanded huge processing power and storage overhead.
    - Some older clips stayed in lower resolutions for a while. The site prioritized popular or newly uploaded videos for conversion, gradually tackling the back catalog.

By the end of 2008, the shift toward higher-quality options was well underway. Though Flash remained the main container for playback, the underlying video encodings improved, laying the groundwork for future HD support.

3. Introduction of HD Playback and Widescreen Format

3.1. Emergence of 720p and 16:9 Ratio

In late 2008, YouTube **officially introduced** support for 720p high-definition video. This move reflected the broader consumer market, where HD camcorders, gaming consoles, and HD television sets were becoming more common.

1. **Widescreen Layout**
    - YouTube updated its default player from the traditional 4:3 aspect ratio (the shape of older TVs) to a 16:9 widescreen layout. This better accommodated HD footage and matched the aspect ratio of modern camcorders.
    - The new layout felt more cinematic. The site's overall design had to adapt, adding black bars to older 4:3 videos or scaling them differently.
2. **Creator Excitement**
    - Ambitious creators embraced 720p wholeheartedly, using higher-end cameras or DSLRs to produce crisper visuals. Tech reviewers, travel vloggers, and short-film directors especially benefited from the improved video fidelity.
    - However, the change raised the bar for production. Some creators worried about being overshadowed if they stuck to older, low-resolution gear. A wave of camera upgrades followed, as many creators deemed HD the new standard.
3. **Viewer Reactions**
    - Users with faster internet connections enjoyed the leap in quality, though some viewers on slower connections struggled with buffering. YouTube responded by offering multiple playback settings (e.g., 360p, 480p, 720p), letting individuals pick what their connection could handle.
    - This multi-resolution approach was a **watershed** for user experience, introducing the concept of toggling playback quality on the fly.

3.2. Technical and Infrastructure Demands

The launch of HD required **significant capacity upgrades**:

1. **Bandwidth Surge**
    - Streaming HD at 720p consumed more data than older resolutions. As YouTube's view counts soared, so did global bandwidth usage. The company invested heavily in data centers and content delivery networks (CDNs) to handle peak traffic.
    - Partnerships with internet service providers (ISPs) became common, aiming to minimize buffering by hosting local caches of popular videos.
2. **Storage Expansion**
    - HD files took up much more disk space, especially when users began uploading hours of footage daily. YouTube multiplied its server infrastructure, leveraging Google's advanced data storage capabilities.
    - The site also refined its transcoding process to compress HD videos efficiently without sacrificing too much visual fidelity.
3. **Global Rollout**
    - Not all regions had the internet speed to handle 720p streaming smoothly. YouTube's adaptive approach (allowing users to choose resolution) helped

- mitigate complaints. Over time, as broadband speeds improved globally, more viewers started opting for HD playback.
- Some early localized versions did not highlight HD as prominently, focusing on stable standard-definition playback for countries where internet speeds lagged. Gradually, HD support reached nearly all localized portals as user demand grew.

The introduction of HD was a turning point that redefined YouTube from a grainy, quick-clip hub to a platform capable of showcasing near-broadcast-level quality—at least by late-2000s standards. This shift laid the groundwork for later expansions into full 1080p, 4K, and beyond.

4. Mobile Viewing and Early App Development

4.1. YouTube Goes Mobile

Even as YouTube thrived on desktops and laptops, the rise of **smartphones** began reshaping internet habits. By 2007, Apple's iPhone and various smartphones running early Android versions hinted at a future where people could watch online videos on the go. YouTube adapted quickly:

1. **Mobile Site**
    - Initially, YouTube created a basic mobile website (m.youtube.com) optimized for small screens and slower cellular networks. It stripped down heavy graphics, focusing on essential features: search, watch, and share.
    - Videos were transcoded to lower bitrates, ensuring they streamed smoothly over 2G or early 3G connections. Quality was modest, but the novelty of watching YouTube anywhere sparked excitement.
2. **Carrier Partnerships**
    - Some phone carriers partnered with YouTube to offer direct links or pre-installed apps on feature phones, though these apps were primitive. Users could watch a limited subset of videos or had to download them partially before playing.
    - As data plans grew more common, carriers saw YouTube usage skyrocket, straining networks unprepared for heavy video streaming.
3. **Early iPhone Integration**
    - Apple's first iPhone (2007) included a dedicated YouTube app that used H.264 streaming. This arrangement preceded full Flash support on iOS (which, in fact, never arrived in a standard way).
    - This iPhone-YouTube synergy helped popularize **mobile video** among early adopters, showcasing a glimpse of a world where people would casually watch YouTube clips in transit, at cafes, or anywhere else.

4.2. Challenges of Mobile Video Delivery

Delivering YouTube on tiny screens with limited connectivity raised new hurdles:

1. **Video Quality vs. Data Caps**
    - Most users had limited monthly data. Streaming too many videos could lead to hefty bills or throttled speeds. YouTube addressed this by automatically detecting

connection speed and adjusting video quality to keep data consumption lower on mobile networks.

- The site also included warning prompts about data usage or recommended connecting via Wi-Fi for extended viewing.

2. **Battery Drain**

    - Prolonged video playback could drain phone batteries quickly. YouTube's engineering teams collaborated with device manufacturers to optimize decoding, balancing performance and power consumption.

    - Some early phone software updates specifically mentioned improved battery life when watching YouTube.

3. **Limited Functionality**

    - The mobile interface often lacked advanced features like detailed channel analytics or in-depth comment threads. Uploading from a phone was possible but clunky. Users had to rely on camera phone recordings, which were automatically compressed, often producing lower-quality clips.

    - Over time, YouTube introduced improvements to allow direct mobile uploads, but in the late 2000s, the user experience was still basic compared to desktop usage.

Despite these growing pains, the introduction of mobile access expanded YouTube's reach, letting viewers tune in at any moment. This anytime-anywhere convenience would eventually become **central** to how people consumed videos, foreshadowing a future dominated by smartphone streaming.

5. Enhanced Discovery and User Engagement Features

5.1. Recommendation Algorithms

From the beginning, YouTube relied on user-driven discovery—featured videos on the homepage, search results, or manual browsing. But as the library ballooned, the site introduced **algorithmic recommendations** to help viewers find relevant clips:

1. **Related Videos Sidebar**

    - One of YouTube's earliest features was the "Related Videos" section, using basic metadata like titles, tags, and descriptions to suggest similar content. This encouraged viewers to keep watching, often hopping from one video to another for extended sessions.

- Over time, the algorithm grew more sophisticated, factoring in watch history, user ratings, and channel subscriptions. The better these recommendations were, the longer people stayed on YouTube.

2. **Personalized Homepage**

   - By 2008, signed-in users saw a homepage tailored to their viewing habits. Recent watch history, likes, or favorites influenced the mix of recommended videos. This personalization aimed to replicate the "serendipity" effect of TV channel surfing, but guided by data.

   - Viewers responded well, often discovering obscure creators or niche interests they might never have found otherwise.

3. **Controversies Over Algorithm**

   - Some creators felt overshadowed if the algorithm didn't favor them. The exact workings were opaque, leading to speculation about how to "game" the system with certain tags or keywords.

   - YouTube tinkered with the algorithm's weighting, trying to balance watch time, user feedback, and diversity of content. Each tweak caused minor upheavals among creators, highlighting how central these automated recommendations were to a channel's growth.

5.2. Interactive Features: Annotations and Polls

To foster user engagement, YouTube released **annotations**—little text boxes or clickable hotspots creators could overlay on their videos:

1. **Annotations as Navigation**
   - Early examples included "Next Episode" links, letting viewers jump to a channel's new video without returning to the main site. This gave comedic web series or vlogs a better continuity.
   - Creators also used annotations to correct mistakes ("Oops, I meant 2006, not 2005!") or to add jokes and side comments in the middle of a clip.
2. **Calls to Action**
   - Many used annotations to encourage watchers to "Subscribe," "Like," or "Comment below." This direct prompting was new in online video, giving creators a tool to build stronger viewer relationships.
   - Some creative projects turned annotations into choose-your-adventure style branching, letting viewers select different outcomes or story paths.
3. **Limitations**
   - Annotations did not work well on mobile, where screens were too small or the annotation system was unsupported. Some found them distracting if overused.

- Over time, the design evolved to be less intrusive, but in these early years, annotations were a novelty that let creators experiment with interactive storytelling.

Though rudimentary by modern standards, these new features hinted at how YouTube aimed to be more than a passive viewing platform. The site encouraged watchers to engage, interact, and shape the experience, expanding the boundaries of what online video could be.

6. Evolving Creator Tools and Analytics

6.1. Video Editor and Basic Editing Functions

As more users recorded and uploaded clips, YouTube sought to help them polish their content with in-platform tools:

1. **Online Video Editor**
    - Launched in a limited capacity, this editor let creators trim the start or end of a clip, splice together multiple uploads, and add simple transitions. It was not as full-featured as desktop editing software but offered a quick fix for minor edits.
    - Many novices appreciated a free, browser-based method to improve their videos without purchasing expensive software.
2. **Annotations and Overlays**
    - Besides the separate annotation feature, the editor introduced text overlays or subtitles. Creators could add simple credits or disclaimers.
    - Some comedic channels used text overlays for comedic effect—like pop-up commentary or silly "thought bubbles" next to a vlogger's face.
3. **Limitations and Reception**
    - Power users found the online editor slow or lacking advanced capabilities, often preferring offline software.
    - However, newcomers loved the convenience of reordering clips or cutting out awkward pauses without re-uploading an entire video. This democratized video production for casual creators.

6.2. Creator Dashboard and Early Analytics

By late 2007, YouTube introduced a **"Creator Dashboard"** with basic analytics. This allowed channel owners to see data such as:

1. **View Counts and Demographics**
    - Creators could track total views, see daily or monthly fluctuations, and look at top countries or cities. This information helped them understand which audience segments they reached.
    - For some, seeing large international audiences was a surprise—driving them to add subtitles or greet global fans.
2. **Engagement Metrics**
    - Early stats included likes, favorites, comments, and five-star ratings. Creators got a sense of viewer sentiment.

    - Over time, the site introduced "retention" metrics, although these were initially simplistic. The ability to see if viewers dropped off halfway through a video helped creators refine pacing or content structure.
3. **Subscriber Growth**
    - Channels gained insights into how many subscribers joined or unsubscribed in a given period. This metric mattered for creators aiming to build a loyal fanbase.
    - Some creators tested different styles or topics, watching analytics to see which videos triggered subscription spikes.

While limited compared to modern YouTube Analytics, these initial tools gave creators a glimpse of professional-level data. They learned to treat channels like small businesses—monitoring audience growth, engagement, and content performance. This data-driven approach influenced content decisions, fueling the evolution of more polished, viewer-friendly videos.

7. Addressing Site Reliability and Performance

7.1. Infrastructure Scaling

Behind the scenes, one of YouTube's greatest challenges was ensuring stable, fast access:

1. **Server Farms and CDNs**
    - Google's acquisition brought massive data center resources. YouTube used Google's global network to distribute content, placing servers in strategic locations to reduce latency.
    - Content Delivery Networks cached popular or trending videos, so viewers in Europe, Asia, or South America could access local copies rather than pulling from a single central server.
2. **Load Balancing and Redundancies**
    - As traffic soared, engineers devised load-balancing algorithms to share the incoming requests among multiple servers. If one cluster neared capacity, new requests redirected to another.
    - This system needed constant tweaking, especially during spikes from viral hits or special events, like a major sports highlight or a presidential debate clip. YouTube prided itself on rarely crashing despite massive surges.
3. **Database Optimization**
    - Tracking billions of video views, comments, and user interactions required advanced database setups. Google's big-data expertise proved invaluable, implementing distributed storage solutions that could handle the read/write volumes.
    - Occasional site maintenance windows or brief errors did occur, but overall reliability improved significantly after 2006, when Google's infrastructure began powering critical YouTube functions.

7.2. Playback Performance and Buffering

Smooth playback was essential for user satisfaction:

1. **Adaptive Bitrate Streaming (Early Steps)**
    - YouTube experimented with methods to adapt the bitrate based on a viewer's connection speed. Though not as refined as modern adaptive streaming, it helped prevent endless buffering for slower connections while still offering HD for those with faster speeds.
    - This technology approach was partly borrowed from protocols used by other streaming services, though YouTube developed its own systems tailored to large-scale user-generated content.
2. **User Feedback**
    - The site introduced basic feedback forms for buffering or playback issues, letting engineers identify trouble spots, perhaps a certain ISP or region.
    - If a country or city had repeated complaints, YouTube partnered with local ISPs to negotiate peering agreements, aiming to route traffic more efficiently.
3. **Mobile Network Challenges**
    - On mobile connections, buffering was more frequent due to 2G or 3G constraints. YouTube's design included smaller default resolutions for mobile, but users could forcibly select higher quality if they wished—often leading to lag. This toggling gave them choice, albeit with possible frustration.
    - Over time, the platform introduced incremental improvements, but the notion of fully seamless mobile HD streaming was still a few years away.

Ensuring consistent playback, especially across an expanding global audience, demanded constant innovation. From re-encoding older videos in better formats to developing smart caching solutions, YouTube's engineering teams invested heavily to keep the site speedy and dependable, thus retaining user trust.

CHAPTER 15: THE GROWTH OF PARTNERSHIPS AND MONETIZATION

---

1. Introduction: From Free Service to Revenue Generator

During YouTube's first few years (2005–2007), the site operated largely without a formal plan for making money. The founders, along with early investors, had focused on attracting users and building a global library of videos rather than seeking immediate profits. However, by 2007 and 2008, the high operational costs—especially bandwidth and storage—made **monetization** a pressing issue. At the same time, YouTube recognized that many creators spent significant time and resources producing videos. Offering creators a chance to earn money would both **reward loyalty** and encourage higher-quality uploads.

In this chapter, we will explore how YouTube developed partnerships with advertisers, media companies, and creators to establish a workable revenue model. We will see how YouTube began introducing ads, negotiated with content owners for licensing agreements, and eventually rolled out early forms of the **Partner Program**—a turning point in user-generated content. We will also investigate the initial reactions from viewers and creators, highlighting the **challenges** of balancing user satisfaction with commercial interests. By the end of this period, YouTube would move beyond a purely user-driven platform into a **multi-layered ecosystem** that combined grassroots creativity with growing corporate relationships.

2. The First Steps into Advertising

2.1. Banner Ads and Display Advertising

In YouTube's earliest days, any ads on the site were extremely minimal. The founders worried that too many advertisements might drive away users, especially at a time when the platform was still building its reputation. The shift toward **display advertising** began gradually:

1. **Banner Ads on the Homepage**
    - Sometime in late 2006 and early 2007, YouTube started placing modest banner ads on its main landing page. These ads were often for tech products or upcoming movie releases, typical for internet display ads at the time.
    - While some users grumbled, the banners were relatively unobtrusive, and the site's massive white background left space for these ads without interrupting the user experience.

2. **Sponsored Video Boxes**
    - YouTube also tested small "Sponsored Videos" modules on the homepage or in the sidebar. These highlighted certain clips paid for by advertisers or corporate content owners.
    - Early sponsors included entertainment companies promoting movie trailers or short TV show previews. The engagement was moderate, but it signaled a new approach: YouTube could **feature** certain videos for a fee.
3. **User Reactions**
    - Most viewers were accustomed to banner ads from browsing other websites, so the initial blowback was mild compared to what might have happened if YouTube launched aggressive, in-video advertising right away.
    - Importantly, the ads did not run **over** user-generated content. This made the presence of banners easier to accept, though it did not generate major revenue.

While these early experiments helped pay a fraction of hosting bills, it was clear that **banner ads alone** would not cover YouTube's rapidly escalating costs. The leadership knew they needed a more robust system to tap into the site's huge viewing population.

2.2. Google's Influence on Ad Strategy

After Google acquired YouTube in late 2006, the platform gained access to **Google's vast advertising network** and expertise, primarily from AdSense and AdWords. However, placing standard text ads on videos was not as straightforward as monetizing search results:

1. **AdWords/AdSense Integration**
    - Google's AdSense program was strong in text-based contexts—like search pages or websites with articles. Video was different. How do you deliver relevant ads to a clip of a cat playing piano, or a short vlog about weekend plans?
    - Google's engineering and ad-sales teams collaborated with YouTube staff to develop ways to **scan video metadata** (titles, tags, descriptions) and user behavior, then serve relevant ads. This was a **nascent** technology back then, but laid the foundation for better ad targeting.
2. **Concern About User Experience**
    - Google executives recognized that YouTube's success came from its user-friendliness. They worried about scaring viewers off with intrusive ads. This

approach shaped the design of early ad formats, which aimed to be **low-impact** while still generating revenue.

- Some prototypes for pre-roll and mid-roll ads were tested behind closed doors, but the leadership decided to move slowly, aware that long, unskippable ads could harm watch time and user goodwill.

3. **Balancing Content Types**
   - Another hurdle was figuring out how to handle user-generated content vs. professional content. Advertisers hesitated to place ads on random home videos without controls over brand safety.
   - On the flipside, major media partners uploading official clips wanted a share of ad revenue. This tension guided YouTube to treat certain videos as "premium," offering advertisers a **safer** environment, while user-generated content remained less monetizable in the short term.

In the end, Google's backing gave YouTube the **time** and **resources** to experiment with different advertising models. Banner ads continued, but the company prepared to introduce more sophisticated ad placements, eventually leading to in-video overlay ads and beyond.

3. Partnerships with Traditional Media and Brands

3.1. The Need for Professional Content

Beyond user uploads, YouTube saw potential in hosting **official content** from TV networks, film studios, record labels, and other entertainment producers. These partnerships served two purposes:

1. **Enhance Legitimacy**: Bringing high-profile, recognizable content to YouTube improved its reputation. People could watch official music videos or TV show clips, not just shaky home recordings.
2. **Attract Advertisers**: Advertisers felt safer placing ads on content from well-known media brands, reducing the chance of their message appearing next to a controversial or offensive video.

3.2. Landmark Deals and Content Licenses

As early as 2007, YouTube struck deals with some large content owners:

1. **Music Labels**

    - Universal Music Group, Sony BMG, and Warner Music were among the first major labels to experiment with official music video uploads on YouTube. They recognized the platform's massive audience could drive song downloads or album sales.

    - In return, they demanded a share of ad revenue when their videos played. This arrangement helped YouTube mitigate accusations of rampant piracy, though it required complicated negotiations.

2. **Television Networks**

    - Some networks, like CBS or BBC, created **official channels** showcasing short clips or highlights from their shows. They might post comedic sketches, news segments, or behind-the-scenes content.

    - These networks earned partial ad revenue, while YouTube benefited from a more diverse content library. Over time, smaller channels or local stations also joined, each seeking to tap the site's reach.

3. **Film Studios**

    Hollywood studios saw YouTube as a promotional vehicle for upcoming movies. They uploaded trailers and teasers, occasionally paying for "featured video" placement.

    Long-form films remained rare due to licensing issues, but short clips and behind-the-scenes featurettes appeared more frequently, building hype for new releases.

These partnerships, though often complicated and prone to legal fine print, **transformed** YouTube from a purely user-generated environment into a hybrid platform that blended grassroots clips with professional entertainment. It also paved the way for bigger brand involvement, which led to new ad revenue streams.

3.3. Early Brand Channels and Sponsorship

Alongside media partnerships, large consumer brands discovered they could directly **engage** customers on YouTube:

1. **Brand Channels**

    - Companies like Coca-Cola, Nike, and Red Bull launched dedicated YouTube channels to share commercials, behind-the-scenes spots, or brand-sponsored events. This gave them a permanent presence on the site, rather than relying solely on purchased ad placements.

- Some brand channels experimented with exclusive content, like mini-web series or user-submitted contests. This approach blurred the line between advertising and entertainment, a trend that would grow in the coming years.

2. **Branded Content with Creators**

   - Though still in its infancy, a few forward-thinking brands teamed up with popular YouTubers for sponsored videos. For instance, a comedic vlogger might incorporate a soft-drink product into a sketch, or a tech reviewer might unbox a new gadget for a sponsored fee.

   - Policies around disclosure were not as strict as they would become later, so the practice was sometimes murky. Nonetheless, these early brand-creator collaborations offered a glimpse into the **influencer marketing** model that would later explode in popularity.

3. **User Response**

   - Viewers often accepted brand channels or branded content if it was **entertaining**. Ads that felt forced or misleading drew criticism. Some users disliked the commercialization, seeing it as a deviation from YouTube's grassroots ethos.

   - Despite pockets of resistance, many recognized that brand sponsorship could improve production quality and allow creators to focus more on making content.

In sum, these partnerships ushered in a new phase where YouTube became a prime venue for **commercial outreach**, not just a platform for random videos. This shift raised questions about how the site would balance corporate interests and user freedom—tensions that would shape its evolving policies and monetization tools.

4. The Birth of the YouTube Partner Program

4.1. Rationale for Sharing Revenue with Creators

One of YouTube's most significant milestones was the launch of the **Partner Program**, which allowed select creators to earn money from ads placed on or around their videos. Before this, only major media partners or large content owners typically received direct ad revenue. But as user-generated videos became a driving force for watch time, YouTube realized it needed to **incentivize** top creators to stay on the platform.

1. **Encourage Quality Content**
    - Sharing revenue rewarded creators who invested time, skill, and resources in their videos. This helped shift user-generated content from casual "webcam rants" toward more polished productions that could draw bigger audiences.
    - Creators with consistent uploads and loyal subscribers began to see YouTube as a potential career path or at least a side hustle.
2. **Reduce Copyright Violations**
    - If creators knew they could earn money from original work, they were less inclined to rely on copyrighted TV clips or music. This, in turn, helped reduce legal headaches for YouTube.
    - Monetization eligibility also required compliance with terms of service—another way to nudge users toward respecting guidelines and intellectual property rights.
3. **Strengthen Community Loyalty**
    - Creators who felt appreciated and compensated by YouTube often reinvested in better equipment or more ambitious projects. This boosted overall content quality.
    - The site's sense of community also deepened, as creators who once relied on random donations or brand deals now had a more official channel for revenue. They could point to real monthly earnings, inspiring others to follow suit.

Thus, the Partner Program aligned YouTube's interests with those of its most dedicated creators, setting the stage for a new breed of content entrepreneurs.

4.2. Selection Process and Requirements

In the early phases of the Partner Program (circa 2007–2008), not everyone could join. YouTube handpicked or invited channels that met certain criteria:

1. **Minimum View Threshold**
    - Creators typically needed a **significant** number of views and subscribers to prove they had an audience. While YouTube never disclosed exact numbers publicly, rumor suggested tens or hundreds of thousands of views were necessary for consideration.
    - This approach ensured that ads ran on content with established popularity, giving advertisers a sense of brand safety and better ROI.

2. **No Copyright Strikes**

    - Channels had to maintain a clean record regarding copyright violations or other rule-breaking. Repeated DMCA takedowns or guideline strikes disqualified a creator.

    - This requirement encouraged creators to make original or licensed content, thereby supporting YouTube's stance against piracy.

3. **Professional Approach**

    - Many early partners were creators who showed consistent quality, a recognizable format, and active engagement with viewers. YouTube wanted to highlight them as examples of what "professional user-generated content" could look like.

    - Some comedic sketch groups, tech reviewers, and educational channels fit this mold, often with regularly scheduled uploads.

Once accepted, partners received a portion of ad revenue from their videos. Though exact percentages remained confidential, many speculated that YouTube took a significant cut while still offering creators a meaningful new income stream.

4.3. Creator Reactions and Early Success Stories

For the first wave of YouTube partners, the program was a **game-changer**:

1. **Turning Hobbies into Income**

    - Many who started posting videos as a casual hobby suddenly found themselves making enough money to upgrade equipment, dedicate more hours to content, or even quit day jobs.

    - This possibility of earning a living through YouTube inspired a surge of new creators aiming to replicate that success.

2. **Transparency Issues**

    - YouTube was guarded about how earnings were calculated, beyond general talk of "revenue shares." Creators saw a monthly AdSense payout but lacked detailed breakdowns of how certain videos performed or how ads were priced.

    - Some partners publicly speculated about eCPM (effective cost per thousand views) or rumored rates. The lack of clarity sometimes caused frustration, as partners sought more data to optimize content.

3. **Rise of the YouTube Personality**

    - With a steady revenue stream, some creators refined their on-camera presence, developed catchphrases, or introduced recurring segments—mirroring the style of television hosts.
    - Fans noticed higher production values and more frequent uploads. As the site matured, more viewers saw YouTube channels as legitimate entertainment sources, akin to mini TV stations.

By the end of 2008, the Partner Program was still limited to a fraction of the creator base, but its existence signaled a fundamental shift: **YouTube was willing to invest** in everyday people, not just big media studios. This development foreshadowed an era where certain individuals, known as "YouTubers," would become some of the platform's biggest draws.

5. The Introduction of In-Video Ads and Overlay Formats

5.1. Overlay Ads vs. Pre-Roll

While banners and sponsored videos were straightforward, YouTube continued testing new ways to place ads **within** the video frame:

1. **In-Video Overlay**

    - One early experiment placed a semi-transparent overlay at the bottom of the video player after a few seconds of playback. The overlay typically displayed a small ad or clickable link. Viewers could close it if they found it distracting.
    - This format was less disruptive than a pre-roll ad that delayed viewing. It allowed watchers immediate access to the video's content, with the ad gently introduced later.

2. **Short Pre-Roll Ads**

    - YouTube also tested short pre-roll ads (five to fifteen seconds) on select partner content. However, many creators and viewers voiced concerns about user experience, especially for short videos where a 15-second ad might feel too long.
    - Over time, a compromise emerged: unskippable pre-roll only for longer or high-profile videos. Shorter videos often used overlays instead. This approach tried to keep the site feeling "fast and fun" while still generating revenue.

3. **Advertiser Feedback**

    - Many brands preferred pre-roll ads because they guaranteed viewer exposure. Overlays might be ignored or closed immediately. Nonetheless, YouTube believed overlays offered a more user-friendly approach.

    - This tension pushed YouTube to keep iterating, eventually introducing skippable pre-roll formats in later years (beyond the timeframe of this chapter). But the **concept** of balancing brand needs with viewer comfort took root here.

5.2. Effects on Viewers and Creators

When YouTube started placing these new ad formats, responses varied:

1. **Viewer Acceptance**

    - Overlays were generally more accepted than unskippable ads. They didn't block immediate access to content, and users could dismiss them. Some viewers clicked the ads out of curiosity, though many simply ignored them.

    - Certain user polls indicated mild irritation, but not enough to deter people from using YouTube as their primary video site. The novelty of user-generated content still outweighed the annoyance of occasional overlays.

2. **Creator Benefits**

    - Partners saw increased earnings since in-video ads typically commanded better rates than basic banners. A comedic channel with consistent daily uploads might see a noticeable jump in monthly revenue.

    - Some creators worried about the ads' intrusiveness, feeling they could disrupt comedic timing or a viewer's immersion in the video. The site responded by letting creators choose ad placement times, though the tools were basic in the late 2000s.

3. **Continuing Monetization Debate**

    - Purists who loved YouTube's early days—where everything was free of ads—lamented the shift. They accused YouTube of "selling out" or sacrificing user experience for profit.

    - However, many recognized that **ads were necessary** for the platform's survival. The cost of hosting billions of videos and streaming them globally was enormous. Monetization, carefully implemented, kept the service running.

In-video advertising, especially overlays, illustrated YouTube's **progressive approach** to revenue: test small, gather feedback, refine. The site's leadership believed a cautious rollout of ads would preserve the sense of fun and spontaneity that made YouTube successful.

6. Early Controversies and Monetization Roadblocks

6.1. Brand Safety Concerns

As YouTube ramped up ads, advertisers occasionally found their messages appearing alongside inappropriate user-generated content—violent, offensive, or otherwise controversial. This sparked **brand safety** worries:

1. **High-Profile Incidents**
   - A few major advertisers discovered their ads next to extremist or explicit videos, prompting public backlash. Some threatened to pull their campaigns if YouTube couldn't guarantee brand-friendly environments.
   - These situations forced YouTube to implement more robust content filtering, ensuring certain categories of videos had limited or no ads.
2. **Demonetization**
   - When videos were flagged for violating guidelines or containing sensitive topics, YouTube began demonetizing them (removing ads entirely). This practice protected brands but angered some creators who felt they were unfairly targeted.
   - In the late 2000s, demonetization was still rare, applied mainly to clear policy violations or repeated rule-breakers. However, it set a precedent for future expansions of "advertiser-friendly" guidelines.
3. **Partner Reassurances**
   - YouTube tried to reassure advertisers by highlighting official partner channels and carefully reviewing their content. The site also developed "Ad-Friendly" content categories, though these policies were still evolving.
   - Over time, the goal was to reduce the risk of big advertisers boycotting YouTube due to a few bad apples.

6.2. Copyright Disputes over Monetized Videos

Another recurring issue: **copyrighted material** in monetized uploads:

1. **Licensed Music or Clips**

- Some creators used commercial music as background in vlogs or comedic sketches. When ads appeared on these videos, rightsholders demanded compensation, or the videos were taken down.

- YouTube introduced or expanded early forms of the Content ID system, allowing rightsholders to claim ad revenue or block usage. This helped reduce legal friction, but also frustrated creators who mistakenly used short music snippets and lost monetization.

2. **Media Company Grievances**

   - Networks and movie studios that had not partnered with YouTube sometimes found user-uploaded show segments or film scenes generating ad revenue for the uploader. They filed takedown requests or insisted on partial revenue.

   - High-profile lawsuits like Viacom's earlier legal action fueled stricter enforcement. Over time, YouTube refined tools that let content owners choose whether to remove infringing videos or **monetize** them.

3. **Creator Confusion**

   - Many new YouTubers did not fully grasp copyright rules. They assumed that if they found a song online, they could use it. Monetizing such content led to sudden channel strikes or revenue re-routed to the music labels.

   - Gradually, YouTube published clearer guidelines explaining fair use, public domain materials, and how to avoid takedowns. The learning curve was steep, but essential for the platform's monetization to work smoothly.

These copyright and brand safety issues revealed the **fragility** of YouTube's revenue model. The site had to manage a delicate balance between user expression, content owners' rights, and advertiser satisfaction.

7. User-Driven Funding Experiments

7.1. Tip Jars and Third-Party Sponsorships

While ads were the main revenue stream, some creators explored alternative funding methods to reduce dependency on YouTube's ad system:

1. **Tip Jar Concepts**

   - A few creators embedded PayPal donation links or used third-party websites to collect tips from fans. This approach appealed to viewers who wanted to support a channel directly, but it remained a niche practice.

    - YouTube toyed with the idea of integrated tip jars but never fully implemented them during this era, focusing instead on advertising.

2. **Off-Site Sponsorship Platforms**

    - Early crowdfunding or sponsorship sites existed but were not widely integrated with YouTube. Creators sometimes asked fans to support them on external platforms, offering perks or bonus content.

    - Because this was all external, YouTube didn't directly profit or facilitate it, but it influenced how some channels diversified income sources.

3. **In-Video Shout-Outs**

    - Creators occasionally offered sponsor shout-outs or brand mentions to earn money outside official YouTube ads. This was a grey area if not disclosed properly, but it predated formal "paid promotion" tags.

    - These small deals foreshadowed a future wave of influencer marketing, though in the late 2000s, it was largely unregulated or improvised.

Overall, these user-driven funding experiments remained secondary compared to official monetization through YouTube's ad system. Nonetheless, they hinted at the platform's capacity for flexible revenue streams, which many creators would explore more extensively in subsequent years.

CHAPTER 16: THE EMERGENCE OF YOUTUBE STARS

---

1. Introduction: From Hobbyists to Household Names

By 2007 and 2008, YouTube's **Partner Program** and the site's massive viewership created a new class of content creators who rose to prominence as genuine "internet celebrities." Unlike traditional celebrities discovered through TV or film, these YouTubers found fame by posting personal, homegrown videos that resonated with online audiences. Fans subscribed to follow comedic routines, vlogs about daily life, music covers, or specialized content like beauty tutorials and gaming.

This chapter explores the **first wave** of YouTube stars, focusing on how they built large followings, interacted with fans, and carved out new forms of entertainment. We will look at the traits that made them successful in an emerging digital medium, the role of collaboration and community support, and the challenges of sudden online fame. YouTube was no longer just a platform for random short clips; it had become a breeding ground for charismatic, innovative personalities who represented the site's evolving culture and mainstream potential.

2. Early Pioneer Channels and Their Formats

2.1. Sketch Comedy and Group Collaborations

One popular path to YouTube stardom was **sketch comedy**:

1. **Group Channels**

    - Some early comedic hits came from small teams of friends producing short, silly videos. They scripted skits, filmed them in backyards or living rooms, and uploaded them weekly or monthly.

    - These groups often had a defined style or recurring characters. Viewers loved the personal feel—like a neighborhood comedy troupe—and subscribed eagerly.

2. **High-Energy Humor**

    - Hyperactive editing, jump cuts, and fast-paced jokes became a YouTube signature. Channels like **Smosh** (founded by Ian Hecox and Anthony Padilla) combined geek culture references with slapstick humor, rapidly gaining millions of views.

    - Fans found the content relatable, as it felt more like watching friends goof around than polished TV comedy. This authenticity separated them from mainstream acts.

3. **Cross-Promotion and Cameos**

    - Sketch groups occasionally collaborated, cameoing in each other's videos. This cross-pollination of audiences helped each channel grow.

    - A comedic cameo from a well-known YouTuber could drive hundreds of thousands of curious fans to another channel, fostering a supportive network of comedic creators.

Simplicity was part of the charm: minimal budgets, basic cameras, and raw energy proved enough to entertain millions. The comedic wave demonstrated how a shared sense of humor and willingness to experiment could **catapult** ordinary folks to internet fame.

2.2. Personal Vlogs and Authentic Connection

Another major category that produced YouTube stars was the **vlog**—personal video blogging:

1. **Daily or Weekly Journals**

    - Some creators filmed routine updates about their lives, sharing thoughts on current events, relationships, or random daily observations. The "I'm just talking to the camera in my bedroom" vibe attracted audiences who craved genuine human connection.

    - Viewers commented with advice, empathy, or personal stories, turning the channel into a virtual diary with communal feedback.

2. **Emotional Candidness**

    - Vloggers stood out by being open about vulnerabilities—discussing social anxieties, heartbreak, or family issues. This raw honesty was unusual in mass media, where celebrities typically had polished images.

    - Audiences found comfort in seeing real people express emotions unfiltered. This fostered deep loyalty, as fans felt they **knew** the vlogger personally.

3. **Fan Interactions**

    - Through comment sections or private messages, vloggers built a tight-knit community. Some answered viewer questions on-camera, read fan mail, or gave shout-outs.
    - This direct engagement was crucial. Fans felt they had a meaningful relationship with the creator, fueling dedicated followings. As the channel grew, viewers rallied around the vlogger, championing them across social networks.

While comedic sketches might amuse casual passersby, personal vloggers cultivated smaller yet fiercely devoted fan bases. These relationships were a new paradigm in entertainment—less about stage presence, more about **relatability** and consistent communication.

2.3. Music Covers and Original Performances

Music was another major driver of early YouTube stardom:

1. **Cover Artists**

    - Singers and musicians who performed covers of popular songs found surprising popularity, as fans searched for alternate renditions of radio hits.
    - Some added unique spins—playing acoustic guitar versions of hip-hop tracks or creating multi-part vocal harmonies on a single webcam feed. This creativity caught the attention of both fans and music industry insiders.

2. **Bedroom Studios**

    - Because professional studio access was expensive, these artists recorded in bedrooms or garages, using cheap mics and basic editing software. The authenticity of these low-budget setups was part of the appeal.
    - Viewers felt like they were witnessing genuine talent "before it was cool," championing undiscovered singers to help them go viral.

3. **Path to Mainstream Recognition**

    - A handful of music-focused YouTubers saw interest from record labels or booked gigs at real venues. Online success sometimes translated into mainstream exposure—for instance, a spot on a late-night talk show or coverage in a local newspaper.

- This set a precedent: you no longer needed to audition for a TV talent show. If your covers garnered millions of views, the industry took notice.

These three categories—comedy, vlogging, and music—provided distinct **entry points** into YouTube fame. Regardless of style, the unifying factor was an authentic, direct connection with fans, combined with a readiness to produce regular content that felt personal or relatable.

3. Building a Loyal Audience

3.1. Consistency and Scheduling

One trait shared by successful early YouTubers was **regular uploads**:

1. **Weekly Episodes**
    - Some comedic channels labeled new skits as "Episode 1," "Episode 2," etc., mirroring TV format. This gave viewers a reason to check back on specific days.
    - Similarly, vloggers announced daily or weekly schedules, forging a habit for their audience. Knowing a new vlog would appear every Wednesday, for instance, built anticipation.
2. **Predictable Segments**
    - Creators often developed recurring bits, catchphrases, or opening sequences. Fans grew comfortable with the format, akin to a TV show's intro.
    - This routine made viewers feel part of a stable "club," especially if the creator addressed them with a nickname or included inside jokes from previous videos.
3. **Viewers as Stakeholders**
    - By releasing content on schedule, creators demonstrated **commitment** to their audience, who reciprocated by subscribing and waiting for each new video.
    - In comment sections, fans sometimes shaped the next episode's topic or challenges—another reason to stay tuned.

3.2. Engaging Viewers Through Calls to Action

Early YouTubers discovered the power of **asking** fans for participation:

1. **Comments and Ratings**

    - Creators would say, "Leave a comment telling me your thoughts," or "Rate this video if you liked it." Simple instructions boosted engagement, making fans feel their feedback mattered.

    - More comments and ratings also helped videos appear in recommended lists or the site's front page, creating a self-reinforcing loop.

2. **Questions and Polls**

    - Vloggers ended videos with direct questions—"What do you think about topic X?"—leading to lively discussions. Some tallied the best answers in the next video, acknowledging fans' contributions.

    - Though the official "poll" feature was minimal, creative channels used annotations or described how viewers could "vote" by leaving specific keywords in the comments.

3. **Community Challenges**

    - A comedic channel might propose a wacky challenge—like "Do a silly dance in public"—and ask viewers to submit their own video responses. The best entries might feature in a future compilation.

    - These user-submitted challenges fueled a sense of shared fun and co-creation, bridging the gap between the star and the audience.

This interactive approach differed from traditional media, where the audience was passive. On YouTube, creators who embraced **viewer participation** saw faster growth, forging a deeper emotional bond with fans.

3.3. Collabs and Guest Appearances

Collaboration was a **cornerstone** of early YouTube star-building:

1. **Cross-Promoting Audiences**

    - Two comedic channels might co-produce a skit, uploading it in two parts—one on each channel—so fans of both had to visit each channel. This cross-promotion expanded each creator's reach.

- Music channels sometimes teamed up for duets, linking to each other's pages in the description or annotations.

2. **Guest Vloggers**

    - Popular vloggers sometimes swapped channels for a day, introducing each other's audience to a new personality. This "channel swap" created excitement, as fans discovered or rediscovered a collaborator's style.

    - This synergy nurtured a sense of community among top creators. Rather than competing for viewers, many recognized that shared audiences fueled mutual success.

3. **Big Group Projects**

    - Occasionally, multiple YouTubers joined forces for a large-scale event—like a fundraising livestream or a compilation video featuring cameo clips from each participant.

    - These group efforts united fans from many channels, fostering a spirit of unity. The "YouTube community" became a genuine subculture, with top creators referencing each other in jokes or responding to each other's videos.

Such collaborations humanized creators further. Fans saw their favorite YouTubers interacting with one another in spontaneous ways, reinforcing the authenticity that defined early YouTube culture.

4. The Fan-Creator Relationship and Early Fandom

4.1. Fan Meetups and Conventions

As channels grew, creators and fans sought **real-world interactions**:

1. **Informal Gatherings**
    - Some creators announced they would be in a certain city park at a specific time, inviting anyone to come say hello. Dozens or even hundreds of fans showed up, surprising even the creators.
    - These early "meetups" lacked formal organization but offered direct, face-to-face communication. Fans took pictures, asked for autographs, or gave homemade fan art.
2. **Online Forum Coordination**
    - Fans used message boards or Facebook groups to plan carpooling or hotels for meetups, turning them into small events. Creators recognized the potential for larger gatherings in the future.
    - Observers noted how YouTube blurred lines between "celebrity" and "viewer": fans felt creators were peers, accessible and genuine, rather than distant Hollywood stars.
3. **Birth of YouTube-Centric Events**
    - By the late 2000s, a few small-scale conventions or fan events dedicated to YouTube content emerged (e.g., unofficial gatherings called "YouTube Live" or city-specific gatherings). These preluded bigger events that would surface in later years.
    - The success of these gatherings showed how devout the YouTube fandom could be, especially for comedic or vlog personalities who thrived on personal connections.

4.2. Fandom Culture: Artwork, Clips, and Memes

YouTube fans often created **fan art** or derivative clips inspired by their favorite stars:

1. **Fan Channels**
   - Dedicated viewers compiled "best of" moments, highlight reels, or reaction videos celebrating a particular vlogger or comedic group.
   - Sometimes these fan compilations went viral on their own, funneling even more attention to the original channel.
2. **Memes and Catchphrases**
   - If a star repeatedly used a funny phrase, fans adopted it, turning it into an inside joke that spread across comment sections. Some fans even made T-shirts or digital graphics with the slogan.
   - This meme-making ability amplified a creator's presence beyond their videos, as watchers recognized these inside jokes in other corners of the internet.
3. **Community Fan Sites**
   - Hardcore fans built small websites or forums devoted to a single creator. They cataloged episodes, wrote fanfiction, or planned future meetups.
   - Creators sometimes visited these sites, leaving appreciative messages that fueled the fandom further. This two-way relationship was a hallmark of YouTube's culture: both parties shaped each other's experience.

Such passionate fandom was unprecedented for homegrown, internet-based entertainers. People typically associated fan clubs with rock bands or TV actors. On YouTube, the **authenticity** and **interactive** nature of content creation gave fans a unique sense of personal investment.

4.3. Handling Negative Fan Interactions

Not all viewer interactions were positive. With sudden fame came **trolls**, harsh critics, or even stalkers:

1. **Trolling and Cyberbullying**
   - Popular creators attracted negative comments—spammers insulting appearances, personalities, or content quality. Some channels developed thick skins and comedic ways to handle trolls, while others struggled.
   - Blocking features or moderated comment sections helped, but large channels faced a constant influx of hateful or disruptive messages.

2. **Privacy Concerns**
    - When a vlogger shared personal details, fans might track down their real address or phone number. In worst-case scenarios, creators faced doxxing or harassment.
    - Some stars learned to set boundaries: they avoided revealing locations or family details, hoping to maintain a safe personal life offline.
3. **Burnout**
    - The pressure to please fans, keep uploading, and handle negative feedback took a toll on some YouTubers. They took breaks or posted emotional vlogs discussing anxiety or creative fatigue.
    - These struggles reflected the site's unique demands. Creators realized that success also brought high expectations from a global audience that never slept.

Despite these challenges, most YouTube stars persevered, supported by loyal fans who appreciated their authenticity. Their ability to address negative experiences openly—rather than hide them behind PR teams—further deepened viewer empathy and connection.

5. The Role of the YouTube Partner Program in Nurturing Stars

5.1. Financial Support for Creative Ambition

With the Partner Program introduced, dedicated creators now had a **financial incentive** to push boundaries and produce consistent, high-quality content:

1. **Investment in Equipment**
    - Earnings from ads helped fund better cameras, lighting, or editing software, boosting production values. This shift from low-resolution webcam footage to near-semi-professional setups signaled the site's evolution.
    - Some comedic channels rented small studios or built makeshift sets in garages, allowing more elaborate skits or short films.
2. **Experimentation with New Formats**
    - Freed from strict budgets, creators experimented with animations, mini-documentaries, or multi-episode story arcs. Ads covered part of the cost, and enthusiastic fans accepted occasional ad breaks as the price of higher production standards.

- Music channels purchased advanced audio gear, leading to polished covers that rivaled official studio recordings.

3. **Full-Time YouTubers**

   - A small group of top earners realized they could quit traditional jobs. They became "full-time YouTubers," devoting themselves entirely to planning, shooting, and editing.

   - This decision was risky—no one was certain if YouTube fame would last. Yet, early pioneers proved that an independent internet career was possible, sparking hope among countless aspiring creators.

5.2. Creator Branding and Merchandise

As channels flourished financially, some personalities expanded beyond ads:

1. **Channel Branding**

   - YouTubers developed consistent logos, intros, or slogans that appeared on their channel art, video thumbnails, and external social media pages. Branding made them recognizable, bridging the gap between an amateur vlogger and a professional show.

   - This approach also helped them stand out in search results—fans looking for a specific style or vibe recognized the channel's visual identity instantly.

2. **Merchandise**

   - T-shirts, posters, wristbands, or even plush toys representing inside jokes or channel mascots appeared. Creators sold these online or at meetups, boosting income and strengthening fan loyalty.

   - Although the scale was small compared to mainstream celebrities, the direct-to-fan model allowed higher profit margins and personalized designs reflecting channel humor.

3. **Potential Brand Collaborations**

   - With strong branding and large followings, some YouTubers attracted **sponsorship offers** from companies wanting them to demo products or incorporate brand mentions. While formal influencer marketing was still new, these deals offered an extra revenue layer.

- Early brand collaborations paved the way for more sophisticated product placements in future years, though the practice remained informal and unregulated in this timeframe.

Through these methods, top creators not only earned ad revenue but also shaped thriving mini-businesses around their personalities. This synergy of personal brand, merchandise, and sponsorship reflected YouTube's transformation into a **viable entertainment industry** alternative.

6. Cultural Impact of Early YouTube Stars

6.1. Redefining "Celebrity"

The rise of everyday people becoming famous through user-generated content challenged the notion of stardom:

1. **Ordinary Backgrounds**
    - Many successful YouTubers were students, retail employees, or just individuals with no special connections in media. Their humble backgrounds made them more relatable than traditional celebrities who often came from auditions, agencies, or nepotism.
    - Fans admired their authenticity: "If they can do it, maybe I can too," became a common sentiment.
2. **Interactive Visibility**
    - Unlike movie stars protected by publicists, YouTubers were accessible in comment sections, live chats, or social media. Fans could actually talk to them.
    - This closeness fostered intense loyalty, though it also meant creators had to handle direct criticism or invasive questions. There was no protective barrier found in conventional stardom.
3. **Grassroots Appeal**
    - Early YouTube stars championed the idea that genuine talent or humor could shine without big budgets or gatekeepers. They represented the democratization of media—anyone with an idea and a camera could try to succeed.
    - This "rags-to-riches" narrative fueled the platform's allure, attracting more aspiring creators who believed YouTube was an open pipeline to recognition.

6.2. Influence on Mainstream Media

As these internet personalities captured large audiences, mainstream media began to notice:

1. **Guest Appearances on TV**
   - Certain comedic channels or vloggers were invited onto morning shows or talk programs to discuss their viral hits. Audiences unfamiliar with YouTube were intrigued by these self-made celebrities.
   - Some YouTubers performed comedic sketches or sang live on TV, bridging the gap between digital fame and traditional entertainment.
2. **Hollywood Interest**
   - In a few cases, managers or small production companies scouted YouTube stars for potential roles in commercials or minor TV appearances. The idea of "internet fame to Hollywood" was new but evolving.
   - However, many YouTubers hesitated to fully embrace Hollywood, preferring creative control and direct fan relationships. This tension underscored YouTube's unique ecosystem where creators had autonomy rarely seen in mainstream media.
3. **Impact on Content Trends**
   - The success of short, snackable comedic bits and vlog-style monologues influenced TV networks to produce similarly brief, web-friendly skits. Some established comedians tested out YouTube to gauge audience reaction before pitching TV pilots.
   - Advertisers also realized the power of relatable personalities in short segments, a concept that would shape modern digital marketing.

Thus, YouTube stars were not just a novelty—they actively shaped cultural and media conversations, demonstrating the viability of a new, decentralized model of content creation and fame.

7. Challenges of Sustaining YouTube Stardom

7.1. Creative Burnout and Pressure

As channels scaled, creators faced **constant pressure**:

1. **Demand for New Content**

- Many fans expected daily or weekly uploads. Slowing down risked losing momentum or unsubscribers. The stress of churning out fresh ideas could lead to burnout or diminishing quality.
- Some comedic groups parted ways due to creative differences or exhaustion. Viewers lamented these breakups, revealing how close fans felt to the entire creative process.

2. **Financial Instability**
   - Ad revenue was unpredictable, fluctuating with the algorithm, viewer engagement, or advertiser budgets. A dip in views could mean a big drop in earnings.
   - Some YouTubers worried about longevity—would their comedic shtick last, or would audiences move on? This uncertainty drove some to diversify income, branch into side ventures, or even shift to mainstream media roles .
3. **Public Scrutiny**
   - Internet fame brought intense scrutiny from fans who documented every slip-up or rumor. Minor controversies could spark large backlash.
   - Channels that lost their "relatable" edge or became embroiled in scandal sometimes saw steep declines in popularity. The internet's memory was long, and rebranding after a public mistake was difficult.

7.2. Platform Changes and Algorithm Shifts

YouTube's evolving algorithms and features also impacted star creators:

1. **Altered Recommendation Systems**
   - Small tweaks to how videos were suggested could drastically affect a channel's traffic. Creators scrambled to decipher the changes—some thrived, others struggled to maintain growth.
   - This gave YouTube immense power: with no guaranteed rules, creators lived at the mercy of algorithmic shifts.
2. **Competition from Newcomers**
   - As YouTube soared in popularity, thousands of aspiring creators entered the scene daily. Established YouTubers had a head start, but new, innovative channels could quickly go viral, stealing attention.

- Maintaining top status required continual evolution, new ideas, or collaborations to stay relevant in a fast-moving environment.

3. **Ad Policy Updates**

    - Stricter brand safety guidelines sometimes demonetized edgy comedic content that had once been profitable. Partners had to adapt or risk losing their revenue streams.

    - This forced creators to self-censor or pivot to safer topics—leading to debates about creative freedom vs. advertiser interests.

In short, achieving YouTube stardom was one challenge—**sustaining it** was another. Yet many early creators managed to adapt, either by diversifying content, building strong fan bases, or negotiating external deals that secured a stable income.

CHAPTER 17: THE EARLY INFLUENCE ON TRADITIONAL MEDIA

1. Introduction: Old Media Meets a New Platform

By 2007–2008, YouTube had already become a household name among internet users, boasting millions of daily video views. Traditional media industries—television networks, film studios, newspapers, and radio stations—were accustomed to being the primary sources of entertainment and news. But now they found themselves looking at an online video platform that attracted vast audiences with user-generated content. This new environment posed questions:

- Would younger viewers abandon traditional TV in favor of online video?
- Could established media harness YouTube's popularity for their own benefit?
- What kind of **relationship** would develop between YouTube and the big players of film, TV, and print?

This chapter explores how mainstream media first reacted to YouTube, from skepticism to eventual collaboration. We will see how television networks sought new ways to distribute clips and how film studios leveraged the platform for promotion. We also examine early instances of print and radio referencing YouTube content. Ultimately, YouTube's influence on traditional media would prove a two-way street: major networks adopted aspects of YouTube's style, while YouTube gained prestige through official partnerships with established names.

2. Traditional Television's Initial Reactions

2.1. Skepticism and Fear of Cannibalization

In the mid-2000s, television executives viewed the rise of YouTube with **mixed feelings**:

1. **Disruption Concerns**
    - TV networks worried that if full episodes or popular show segments were freely available on YouTube, viewers would skip broadcast airings. This threatened advertising revenue, which relied on scheduled programming.

- There was also fear of losing control over how content was presented. Television had always had strict licensing and regional broadcast rights. YouTube's global, user-uploaded model bypassed these norms.

2. **Questions About Quality**

    - Many TV producers dismissed user-generated content as amateurish, comparing YouTube's shaky home videos unfavorably to polished TV programs.

    - They assumed viewers would continue valuing big-budget shows over grainy, low-budget uploads. Yet viral clips on YouTube suggested otherwise—authenticity and humor often trumped production value, forcing networks to reassess viewer preferences.

3. **Copyright and Legal Tensions**

    - Many networks sent **takedown notices** en masse, demanding YouTube remove copyrighted content from popular shows like "Saturday Night Live," "The Simpsons," or "CSI." They saw YouTube as an infringement hub.

    - In some instances, entire episodes were uploaded in multiple parts. Legal teams for networks spent countless hours identifying these clips. This aggressive stance—"remove it all"—reflected the anxiety that YouTube threatened broadcast exclusivity.

These initial responses highlighted the gap between an emerging digital video culture and the traditional TV business model. Yet, even as networks fought unauthorized uploads, they couldn't ignore YouTube's massive audience.

2.2. Quiet Experimentation with Official Clips

Despite public resistance, certain TV networks explored ways to **leverage** YouTube's reach:

1. **Short Highlight Reels**

    - Some networks tested posting short, **official** highlight clips from talk shows or late-night comedy skits. They reasoned that short segments could act as teasers, driving fans to watch full episodes on TV or network websites.

    - Early examples included short comedic bits from "The Daily Show" or "The Tonight Show," posted on official YouTube channels. The networks retained control of these uploads, ensuring brand-safe presentation.

2. **Preview Promotions**

    - New show pilots or big season premieres got extra buzz if a snippet was made available on YouTube. This was akin to running extended trailers, hoping viral sharing would drive up live viewership.
    - Some marketing teams embedded links or end cards directing watchers to official network pages or reminding them of upcoming broadcast times.

3. **Selective Monetization**

    - Networks that recognized the potential for ad revenue agreed to let YouTube place ads on these official uploads, then split the earnings. This was far more attractive than viewers watching pirated versions.
    - While the amounts were modest initially, the networks liked having **some** revenue stream rather than zero. This arrangement also gave them partial control over the content environment, mitigating brand safety worries.

These cautious steps signaled a shift: even as networks battled unauthorized clips, they began to see YouTube as a **promotional ally**, especially for reaching younger demographics who spent more time online.

2.3. Impact on Broadcast Scheduling

YouTube's culture of **on-demand** viewing pressured TV networks to rethink how they scheduled and distributed shows:

1. **Rethinking Exclusivity Windows**

    - Previously, networks guarded episodes behind strict broadcast schedules. But with viewers flocking to YouTube for highlights, networks started uploading official segments soon after airing.
    - Some networks used these quick clips to build **next-day buzz**—for instance, a musical performance on a late show might appear on YouTube by morning, capturing social media conversations while they were still fresh.

2. **Clip-Sharing on News Programs**

    - News outlets began referencing YouTube hits during broadcasts, showing short bits of viral videos. This practice introduced the notion of "If you missed it on the internet, catch it here on TV," reversing the usual flow.

   - Producers recognized that younger audiences discovered newsworthy or humorous moments on YouTube first. TV stations then had to keep up by showcasing those same moments. The synergy started bridging old and new media.

3. **Evolving Viewer Habits**

   - As fans embraced "time-shifted" viewing online, TV networks faced falling live ratings. The presence of official or unofficial YouTube clips meant viewers could watch comedic or news segments at their convenience rather than tuning in at a specific hour.

   - This trend pushed networks to explore **multi-platform strategies**, such as streaming episodes on network websites or digital marketplaces. Although not fully developed at that time, the seeds of modern streaming models were already visible.

Thus, YouTube did more than just challenge broadcast exclusivity. It **catalyzed** new thinking around how TV programs reached the public and how viewers engaged with them post-broadcast. Over time, these changes would redefine the relationship between TV and digital platforms.

3. Film Industry Embraces Online Trailers

3.1. Movie Studios Discover the "Viral Trailer"

Hollywood studios also recognized YouTube's potential, especially for **trailer promotion**:

1. **Official Trailer Channels**

   - Some studios launched their own YouTube channels dedicated to upcoming movies. They posted trailers, teaser clips, and behind-the-scenes footage, taking advantage of YouTube's easy embedding on external websites.

   - This approach replaced older methods (like QuickTime downloads on official movie sites), making it simpler for fans to watch and share clips across social media or email.

2. **Viral Marketing Campaigns**

   - Certain blockbusters used YouTube as a **viral marketing** tool. Cryptic teaser videos or mini-teasers seeded curiosity among fans. People debated them in comment sections, fueling hype.

- Horror or science-fiction films, in particular, thrived on cryptic campaigns. They'd release short, eerie clips hinting at the plot. Viewers speculated in fan forums, driving word-of-mouth.

3. **Extended Reach and Buzz**

   - Prior to YouTube, studios paid for TV spots or theater previews. Online distribution let them gauge audience reaction instantly through comments and view counts.

   - Positive reception or high view counts became a bragging point in press releases—"This trailer garnered 2 million views in 24 hours." Marketing teams realized that YouTube metrics could demonstrate pre-release interest.

This synergy helped the film industry see YouTube as more than a threat. Although they remained vigilant about unauthorized uploads of full scenes, official marketing content thrived on the platform, letting studios tap into a massive, engaged audience cost-effectively.

3.2. Clashes over Copyrighted Scenes

Nevertheless, the film studios' relationship with YouTube had **bumps**:

1. **Movie Clips vs. Promotional Materials**

   - Studios wanted control over which scenes appeared online. While short trailers were fine, random user-uploaded movie clips might reveal spoilers or reduce the impetus to buy tickets.

   - Companies filed takedown notices for extended scenes or entire segments. Disputes erupted over fair use, especially when fans used movie clips for commentary or parodies.

2. **Limited Monetization Options**

   - Some studios demanded that if a user posted a copyrighted scene, they (the studio) should receive ad revenue or the clip should be removed. Early Content ID tools offered partial solutions, but disagreements persisted about how long or how many movie segments were permissible.

   - In a few cases, studios recognized fan-made tributes could be beneficial, so they allowed them to remain online, claiming partial monetization rather than demanding a takedown. This flexible approach emerged gradually as studios tested the platform's promotional upsides.

3. **Public Perception**

    - Big studios that aggressively removed clips risked alienating fans, who saw them as "anti-fan." Others that allowed mild usage of scenes earned goodwill, with viewers praising them for embracing digital culture.

    - Over time, the film industry, like TV networks, discovered that a balanced approach—allowing some user creativity while policing major infractions—was more beneficial than blanket removal.

Hence, while official trailers and marketing stunts thrived, the question of user-uploaded movie clips became a **source of tension**. The film industry grappled with balancing promotion against unauthorized distribution, mirroring TV's earlier copyright battles.

4. Print Media and Radio Integrate YouTube Content

4.1. Newspapers Referencing Viral Videos

As online activity soared, print outlets also began **citing YouTube** in stories:

Human-Interest Coverage

- Local newspapers frequently ran articles on "Viral Video of the Week," featuring heartwarming or bizarre YouTube clips. This gave older or less tech-savvy readers insight into internet phenomena.

- These articles often included instructions: "Search for 'funny dog dances salsa' on YouTube to find the clip." It marked an unusual shift where print led readers to online video.

Editorial Commentary

- Opinion columnists occasionally analyzed the cultural significance of popular videos—like a comedic political parody or an amateur music cover. This bridged the gap between digital youth culture and mainstream readers.

- Some newspapers debated whether YouTube signaled the decline of long-form journalism, as younger audiences spent more time on short, entertaining videos. Others argued that viral videos could complement traditional reporting by offering quick, visual insights.

Embedding in Online Editions

- Many newspapers launched their own websites with article pages that embedded relevant YouTube clips. For instance, a story about a local teen's singing success would include the teen's YouTube performance.
- Though embedding was not always flawless in early years, it offered synergy between text reporting and viral video content.

These interactions exposed new demographics to YouTube, including older generations who learned about viral clips through newspaper features. In turn, print media extended their stories beyond static text, harnessing YouTube's rich visual dimension.

4.2. Radio Stations Promote YouTube Discoveries

Radio hosts also saw potential in YouTube:

1. **On-Air Discussions**
    - Morning shows or talk-based radio segments discussed trending clips, describing them verbally while encouraging listeners to check them out later on YouTube.
    - DJ chatter about a comedic video often generated interest; fans would later watch, comment, and sometimes credit the station for the tip. This cross-promotion boosted YouTube view counts and gave radio relevant new content to fill airtime.
2. **Guests and Interviews**
    - Some YouTube creators were invited onto radio programs to talk about their viral success. Although purely an audio format, radio recognized the appeal of capturing an internet star's personality for a short interview.
    - Conversely, certain talk shows posted behind-the-scenes or highlight clips on YouTube to attract a younger online audience. This synergy underscored YouTube's growing importance for all media forms, even audio-only.
3. **Listener-Driven Content**
    - Radio stations occasionally asked callers, "What's your favorite recent YouTube clip?" turning segments into crowd-sourced recommendations. The spontaneity mirrored YouTube's user-driven ethos.

    - This practice kept radio content fresh and connected to the new wave of internet memes, bridging the gap between digital video trends and a purely auditory medium.

The radio sector thus found YouTube beneficial for **keeping up with pop culture**. Although the platform itself was visual, radio personalities leveraged it for comedic fodder, interviews, and synergy with listeners. This reflected a growing trend: YouTube was **everywhere**, shaping the content of all types of traditional media outlets.

5. Celebrity Crossovers and Talent Discovery

5.1. YouTubers Appear on Television

In Chapter 16, we touched on how popular creators occasionally made it onto TV. Let's detail how that influenced traditional media:

1. **Late-Night Talk Shows**
    - Some comedic YouTubers were invited to perform a short sketch or demonstrate their unique talents. Late-night hosts recognized that featuring an internet star generated buzz among younger audiences.
    - The synergy often drove more fans to the YouTuber's channel afterward, while also boosting a show's social media visibility.
2. **Reality Talent Competitions**
    - Shows like "America's Got Talent" or "Britain's Got Talent" used YouTube as a scouting tool, spotting potential contestants who'd already built a following online.
    - Judges and producers welcomed these acts because they came with built-in fan bases, translating into higher viewer engagement and votes.
3. **Hosts and Correspondents**
    - A few YouTubers landed roles as special correspondents or guest hosts on smaller cable channels, especially for pop culture or tech-oriented shows. Their on-camera ease and loyal fans made them valuable assets, even if they lacked traditional broadcasting credentials.

Such crossovers eroded the barrier between "internet fame" and "TV fame." Traditional media no longer dismissed YouTube success as fleeting but recognized it as a **legitimate** audience magnet.

5.2. Traditional Celebrities Embrace YouTube

Conversely, established actors, musicians, and comedians realized that **maintaining a YouTube presence** could expand their reach:

1. **Personal Channels**
    - Some film or TV stars created personal YouTube channels to share behind-the-scenes footage or interact with fans. This offered a more candid side of celebrities typically seen only through polished interviews.
    - Fans appreciated the informal vibe, posting thousands of comments. Actors who engaged directly with viewers earned praise for openness.
2. **Music Promotions**
    - Well-known musicians posted official music videos or lyric videos on YouTube, reaping massive view counts. Even older songs found new life among younger listeners.
    - Celebrity-run vlogs or Q&A sessions kept fans updated between album releases, fostering deeper loyalty. YouTube's comment sections became mini fan clubs.
3. **Collaborations with YouTubers**
    - Some mainstream celebrities collaborated with popular YouTube creators to cross into digital-savvy audiences. For example, a famous comedian might appear in a comedic vlogger's video.
    - Such stunts grabbed headlines, with mainstream outlets noting how celebrities were "reaching out to the internet generation" in ways that appealed to younger viewers used to direct interaction with their idols.

This two-way integration marked a turning point. Traditional stars realized they could benefit from YouTube's huge user base, while YouTubers found new legitimacy by associating with mainstream personalities. In effect, YouTube was catalyzing a **media merge** where lines between online and offline stardom blurred.

6. Early Instances of Co-Production

6.1. Joint Web Series

Beyond simple clip-sharing, some traditional media companies experimented with **web series** made specifically for YouTube:

1. **TV Network Spinoffs**
    - A network might create a short comedic series tied loosely to a prime-time show, releasing episodes only on YouTube. This content attracted fans of the main show while giving them exclusive online extras.
    - Low production costs and the ability to measure direct viewer engagement made these spinoffs a low-risk experiment for networks.
2. **Co-Funded Mini-Series**
    - A few small production houses partnered with YouTube to launch exclusive mini-series starring known actors or well-regarded directors. While such projects had limited budgets, they generated excitement for bridging pro-level production with the immediacy of YouTube.
    - These mini-series often teased potential for larger projects, essentially using YouTube as a test market for new creative concepts.
3. **User Interaction**
    - Some co-produced web series encouraged viewers to vote on plot points or endings. This interactive format capitalized on YouTube's comment-driven culture.
    - Though the concept was experimental, it showcased how real-time feedback could shape narrative content—a stark contrast to standard TV, where audience input came only through ratings or post-show surveys.

These early co-productions hinted at a **future** where networks or film companies might create streaming-first titles. While mainstream streaming platforms had not yet taken off, YouTube's foray into original or co-produced content foreshadowed a shift away from linear broadcast models.

6.2. Syndication and Archive Projects

Traditional media outlets also saw YouTube as a potential space to **archive** older shows or segments:

1. **Classic Clips**
    - Networks posted vintage sketches or legendary TV moments from archives. This allowed younger audiences—who never saw the original broadcasts—to discover classic comedy or historical newscasts.

- Seeing these archived clips go viral occasionally boosted nostalgia-driven DVD sales or re-airing interest.

2. **News Archives**

    - Some news organizations uploaded past coverage of major events for educational or commemorative purposes. Although these typically did not generate huge ad revenue, they enhanced the organization's public service image.

    - Teachers or researchers found these archives useful for lesson plans, linking directly to historical footage without relying on paid licensing deals.

3. **Rights and Regional Blocks**

    - Archival efforts often faced rights complications, especially for older shows produced under different contracts. Some archives were blocked in certain countries due to unresolved distribution rights.

    - Despite such hurdles, the archiving of select content on YouTube demonstrated how traditional media recognized the platform as a **repository** for historical broadcasts—an unusual concept just a few years before.

Archival uploads represented a bridging of generational gaps, letting YouTube users sample historical media. This move also reaffirmed that the site served not just ephemeral viral moments but could become a **cultural library** bridging past and present entertainment.

7. Shaping the Future of Media Consumption

7.1. Viewer Expectations of Interactivity

One of YouTube's biggest influences on traditional media was the expectation that **viewers should interact**:

1. **Comment Culture**

    - As people grew accustomed to commenting on YouTube videos, they began expecting more direct feedback avenues for TV content. Networks responded by encouraging live tweeting or setting up official forums.

    - Although not exactly the same as a YouTube comment section, the push toward real-time audience engagement was partially inspired by YouTube's easy conversation model.

2. **Immediate Access and On-Demand**

    - The success of short, shareable clips eroded patience for the old model of waiting a week for a show. This shift nudged TV networks to launch streaming apps or websites hosting episodes soon after broadcast, acknowledging viewers' desire for convenience.

    - Even radio, seeing how YouTube allowed on-demand replay, began publishing podcast versions or highlight reels. The popularity of watch-anytime culture had spread across media fields.

3. **Self-Directed Discovery**

    - YouTube's recommendation algorithms introduced users to content they never sought deliberately. This "browsing by algorithm" or "going down the rabbit hole" replaced channel surfing as a prime discovery method.

    - Traditional media outlets tried replicating this with curated digital catalogs or cross-promoting shows. Over time, big networks would create sophisticated recommendation engines for their own online platforms, taking cues from YouTube's user-driven environment.

Hence, the user-centric, interactive ethos shaped how mainstream outlets provided content. Television, radio, and print realized they had to engage watchers and listeners on multiple fronts, offering flexible, on-demand options rather than rigid schedules.

7.2. Influence on Content Style

In addition to distribution, YouTube's style impacted **how** content was produced:

1. **Short-Form Segments**

    - YouTube's emphasis on brevity and pacing showed that viewers could be hooked in seconds. Television producers responded by creating shorter, punchier segments, especially for comedic or variety shows.

    - Teasers or "cold opens" became more dynamic, mirroring the "get to the point quickly" approach prevalent in viral videos.

2. **Direct-to-Camera Intimacy**

    - The vlog format—someone speaking directly to the camera—became popular in magazine shows or documentary segments. Hosts or reporters started using personal, confessional tones, forging a sense of one-on-one connection with viewers.

- This reduced the formality of traditional presenting styles, bridging the authenticity gap that once separated TV professionals from everyday YouTube creators.

3. **User-Generated Spots**

    - Some TV programs invited viewers to send short videos that might air on the show. This mimicked YouTube's user-driven approach, letting fans see themselves on television.

    - In some cases, entire segments were devoted to user-submitted comedic clips or local talent highlights, turning TV watchers into content contributors—a direct reflection of YouTube's participatory culture.

As a result, the traditional model of top-down broadcasting started to blur: the audience was no longer a passive mass, but a group of potential participants. YouTube's success at democratizing creation and embracing authenticity inspired conventional media to incorporate these traits.

CHAPTER 18: CORPORATE CHANGES AND GROWING PAINS

1. Introduction: The Transition from Startup to Subsidiary

When Google officially acquired YouTube in late 2006, the platform entered a new phase. No longer a small, independent startup, YouTube now had access to Google's vast resources, data centers, and advertising network. Yet, the transition also brought **organizational challenges**. The site's founders—Chad Hurley, Steve Chen, and Jawed Karim (who had already stepped back from day-to-day operations)—faced new realities about scaling infrastructure, coordinating with Google's broader corporate structure, and balancing innovation with compliance and policy concerns.

In this chapter, we explore how YouTube **shifted** from a scrappy disruptor to a more formalized subsidiary under Google's umbrella. We will see how the company expanded its staff, reorganized leadership roles, and adapted internal processes to handle worldwide growth. Alongside these changes came **growing pains**—internal tensions over content moderation, evolving ad policies, international compliance, and efforts to maintain a user-friendly image. By the end of this period, YouTube was no longer just an exciting newcomer but a platform grappling with the realities of success on a global scale.

2. Management and Structural Overhauls

2.1. The Founders' Changing Roles

Chad Hurley, Steve Chen, and Jawed Karim shaped YouTube's original vision. After Google's acquisition:

1. **Chad Hurley as CEO**
    - Chad Hurley retained the CEO title for a while, focusing on **product design** and strategic decisions. However, he was now part of a larger Google leadership hierarchy, reporting to Google executives and coordinating with various Google departments.
    - Over time, Hurley's role became more symbolic, as day-to-day management responsibilities spread among a growing team of vice presidents and directors.
2. **Steve Chen's Technical Focus**
    - Steve Chen took on key responsibilities related to **scaling** YouTube's technology. He worked closely with Google's infrastructure teams to integrate data center expansions, reduce buffering, and refine video encoding processes.
    - Like Hurley, Chen gradually transitioned into a less hands-on role as new engineering managers joined, though he remained the face of YouTube's innovative backend strategies.
3. **Jawed Karim's Departure**
    - Jawed Karim, who had stepped back even before the acquisition, became more of an adviser. He was neither heavily involved in day-to-day decisions nor held a major executive title under Google. He eventually pursued other ventures and educational pursuits.
    - Karim's departure symbolized the shift from a tight-knit founder trio to a broader corporate structure with specialized departments and hundreds of employees.

These leadership transformations reflected YouTube's evolution from an agile, founder-led startup to a subsidiary needing **formal hierarchy** and cross-functional coordination with Google's established teams.

2.2. Integration with Google Divisions

Bringing YouTube fully under Google required **cross-department collaborations**:

1. **Advertising and Monetization Teams**

    - YouTube's emerging ad products merged with Google's AdWords/AdSense staff. They co-developed new formats (like in-video overlays) and refined ad-targeting algorithms.
    - Communication challenges arose: Google employees who specialized in text search ads had to learn about user-generated video environments, brand safety, and content policies.

2. **Legal and Policy Departments**

    - Google's formidable legal team stepped in to handle major lawsuits (e.g., Viacom) and form standardized processes for dealing with DMCA takedowns.
    - YouTube's existing policy folks now had corporate backing for escalations, but they also faced stricter compliance frameworks. This meant more thorough guidelines, training, and documentation.

3. **Infrastructure and Data Centers**

    - YouTube engineering coordinated with Google's infrastructure group to scale servers, CDNs, and global load balancing. The cost of streaming soared, but under Google's umbrella, resources were more readily available.
    - Merging codebases and monitoring systems was not trivial. Some engineers lamented bureaucratic delays, while others appreciated stable budgets and advanced tools.

Overall, these integrations were beneficial but **time-consuming**. Merging a fast-moving startup culture with Google's established processes created friction, yet it gave YouTube the foundation to handle exponential user growth.

2.3. Hiring Sprees and Department Growth

As YouTube's footprint expanded worldwide, so did its staffing needs:

1. **Product and Engineering**

    - Dozens, then hundreds, of new engineers joined to refine the website, recommendation algorithms, mobile apps, and behind-the-scenes encoding tools.

- Product managers specialized in everything from user experience to analytics dashboards for creators. Some came from Google's other divisions, bringing a more structured approach to feature rollouts.

2. **Trust & Safety Teams**

    - Content moderation became critical as YouTube faced rising volumes of flags and reports for hateful, violent, or explicit content. Dedicated "Trust & Safety" teams were formed to develop new guidelines and respond to user or government complaints.

    - This department grew rapidly, hiring staff with language skills and cultural knowledge to handle user flags from diverse global regions.

3. **Business Development and Partnerships**

    - Deeper collaborations with music labels, TV networks, and advertisers required business-savvy professionals. YouTube built teams to negotiate licensing, revenue splits, and sponsor deals.

    - Many staffers came from the entertainment world, bridging the gap between the open YouTube culture and traditional media's structured contracts.

This hiring spree turned YouTube from a small group of generalists into a **multi-department organization** with specialized roles. The founders had to adapt to overseeing managers rather than personally approving every new idea.

3. Policy Evolution and Moderation Challenges

3.1. Growing Pressure for Content Controls

As user uploads soared, so did **controversial content**:

1. **Inappropriate or Offensive Videos**

    - Viewers flagged videos containing extreme violence, harassment, explicit sexual content, or hate speech. While YouTube's original guidelines banned certain categories, enforcement was patchy.

    - Media coverage of shocking clips put pressure on YouTube to tighten policies. Governments worldwide demanded quicker removals, sometimes threatening blocks if offensive content remained accessible.

2. **DMCA Takedowns**

    - Copyright disputes continued to pile up. With more official content deals, YouTube needed to ensure it wasn't hosting infringing uploads. The staff scrambled to process thousands of DMCA notices each week.

    - Rightsholders insisted on faster and more accurate detection, prompting expansions of early Content ID technologies. The system was far from perfect, leading to misflags and frustration among legitimate creators.

3. **Brand Safety Requirements**

    - Major advertisers complained about ads appearing on hateful or extremist videos. YouTube responded by rolling out "advertiser-friendly guidelines," demonetizing or restricting ads on questionable content.

    - Partners that felt unfairly demonetized voiced concerns about transparency. Tensions grew between the site's open ethos and the commercial demands of brand partners.

Thus, YouTube found itself juggling user freedoms, legal obligations, and corporate responsibilities. The once carefree environment of "upload anything" was tempered by more formal, **enforced** rules.

3.2. Refining Community Guidelines

To address these mounting issues, YouTube updated its **Community Guidelines**:

1. **Explicit Ban Categories**

    - New guidelines specified categories like harassment, hate speech, sexual content, and dangerous acts in clearer language. The site began training staff to interpret these rules consistently.

    - This provided a reference for removing blatantly inappropriate videos or comments, though subjective grey areas remained.

2. **Age Restrictions**

    - YouTube introduced stricter age-gating for content deemed inappropriate for minors. Certain flagged videos required users to log in and confirm their age before viewing.

- While this move helped shield younger viewers, many recognized it was easy to bypass by lying about one's birthdate. Still, it symbolized an effort to address concerns about adult content.

3. **Strikes System**

   - For repeated guideline violations, YouTube developed a "strikes" policy. A first strike might block features or remove monetization, escalating to a channel ban if strikes accumulated.
   - Creators complained about overzealous enforcement or unclear rules. The staff tried to refine the process, but confusion persisted, reflecting the complexities of moderating a massive user base.

These policy updates formed a **necessary structure** to manage diverse global content. However, they sparked debates over censorship, fairness, and the risk that YouTube might abandon its free-wheeling culture for a more corporately sanitized environment.

4. International Operations and Regulatory Pressures

4.1. Challenges of Local Laws

In Chapter 13, we examined YouTube's international expansion. That rapid growth led to **regulatory entanglements**:

1. **Local Censorship**

   - Certain governments demanded that politically or culturally sensitive videos be blocked within their territories. YouTube's leadership wrestled with whether to comply partially or risk a total ban in those regions.
   - Google's legal teams guided negotiations, sometimes leading to "geo-blocking" specific videos. Critics accused YouTube of capitulating to censorship; supporters argued partial service was better than none.

2. **Unique Copyright Structures**

   - Each country had different copyright collecting societies, licensing rules, and fair-use interpretations. YouTube's global legal staff navigated patchwork agreements to avoid lawsuits.
   - Some markets had slower progress due to prolonged negotiations. Music licensing remained a frequent stumbling block, with local agencies demanding complex revenue splits or set minimum fees.

3. **Data Localization**

    - A few countries proposed laws requiring user data or servers to reside locally. While not heavily enforced yet, the concept raised logistical questions about storing or duplicating enormous amounts of video data in multiple places.

    - YouTube weighed these requirements against the technical efficiency of centralized infrastructure. This foreshadowed deeper debates about data sovereignty in subsequent years.

Meeting local demands while preserving a relatively uniform global service tested YouTube's adaptability. Each compromise or new law threatened to fragment the platform's user experience if not managed carefully.

4.2. Coordinating with Google's Global Offices

Because Google already operated worldwide, YouTube integrated with **existing regional offices**:

1. **Localized Sales Teams**

    - In Europe, Asia, and Latin America, Google sales reps pitched YouTube ad opportunities to local brands. This synergy boosted ad revenue in non-English-speaking markets.

    - However, these teams needed specialized knowledge about YouTube's unique content environment. Some brand managers remained hesitant, especially regarding user-generated videos.

2. **Country Managers**

    - YouTube hired or appointed local "country managers" to handle marketing, partner outreach, and government relations. These roles were crucial for bridging cultural gaps and ensuring compliance with local norms.

    - Managers also organized local creator events and facilitated major content deals with regional media outlets, continuing the push to bring more professional or mainstream content to the platform.

3. **Translation and Localization**

    - YouTube's interface, help center, and content guidelines needed constant updates in dozens of languages. This was an ongoing project, with a dedicated localization team.

- Automated translations for video titles or descriptions were rudimentary, so staff occasionally recruited volunteers or local agencies to maintain accuracy.

While leveraging Google's infrastructure helped, each new local version of YouTube brought new demands. Balancing user growth with regulatory compliance became an everyday **management challenge**, requiring structured coordination that was unfamiliar to the once small, freewheeling startup.

5. Internal Cultural Shifts

5.1. Startup Spirit vs. Corporate Environment

Longtime YouTube employees sometimes missed the **informal, fast-paced** culture of the early years:

1. **Increased Bureaucracy**
   - Decisions that once took days now required multiple approvals from Google's finance, legal, or product committees. Some developers found the pace frustrating.
   - With more staff, internal communication could be slow or confusing. Employees who thrived on quick turnarounds had to adapt or risk burnout in an environment with more structured processes.
2. **Resource Abundance**
   - On the positive side, the partnership with Google meant no more panicked scrambles for server capacity. Teams had budgets for specialized tools, robust data analysis, and expansions.
   - The new corporate environment also offered better benefits and stability for employees, which improved morale among those who valued consistent career development.
3. **Balancing Innovation and Policy**
   - Product managers found themselves balancing user-friendly features with compliance concerns. A new idea for video sharing or interactive tools might require thorough legal reviews.
   - This tension sometimes slowed radical experiments, though it also protected YouTube from legal missteps. The challenge was to remain innovative while abiding by bigger-company constraints.

Hence, while resources grew, so did overhead and formalities. The close-knit "everyone knows everyone" vibe gave way to departmental silos, typical of a large tech subsidiary. Some staff embraced this professionalization; others longed for earlier spontaneity.

5.2. Developing Creator Relations Teams

As seen in Chapter 15, the Partner Program fueled a surge of professional creators:

1. **Dedicated Creator Liaisons**
   - YouTube established a "Creator Relations" group to provide guidance, handle partner questions, and build a stronger sense of community among top channels.
   - These liaisons advised on best practices for video production, channel branding, and using new features, essentially becoming mentors for aspiring full-time YouTubers.
2. **Workshops and Meetups**
   - The site organized small workshops or local gatherings where partners could learn about new platform tools, ad strategies, and collaborative opportunities.
   - These events often included direct feedback sessions, letting creators voice concerns about monetization, policy, or algorithm changes. Such communication channels were new for a tech platform at the time.
3. **Early Recognition Programs**
   - Some staff proposed awarding "Silver," "Gold," or "Diamond" accolades based on subscriber milestones (though official programs of that nature were still in development phases).
   - The idea was to celebrate achievements and keep creators motivated. This concept later evolved into the well-known Creator Awards, but seeds were planted during these earlier years of corporate changes.

These initiatives highlighted YouTube's realization that creator satisfaction was vital to the site's success. The introduction of official "relations" roles signaled a more structured, **customer service-like** approach, where creators were seen as key stakeholders rather than just random uploaders.

6. Monetization Refinements and Ad Policy Adjustments

6.1. Refining Ad Placement

With millions of monetized videos, YouTube continued **tweaking** how and when ads appeared:

1. **Mid-Roll Ads on Longer Videos**

    - After seeing the success of short overlays and occasional pre-rolls, YouTube tested mid-roll ads for videos exceeding a certain length. This approach resembled TV commercial breaks, but typically only top partners or long-form content creators had access to it.

    - Viewer acceptance varied; some disliked interruptions in the middle of user-generated videos. Yet the potential for higher ad revenue attracted creators, especially those producing episodic or extended content.

2. **Improving Ad Targeting**

    - Teams integrated Google's ad-targeting algorithms more deeply, matching user interests gleaned from search or browsing data with relevant videos.

    - While this boosted ad performance, it also raised privacy questions: how much data was being shared across Google's ecosystem? Public debate on data use was in its infancy, but seeds of concern were sown.

3. **Early Experimentations with Skippable Ads**

    - Although not widely rolled out yet, YouTube tested formats that let viewers skip an ad after a few seconds, only charging advertisers if viewers watched the entire spot.

    - This compromise aimed to keep user satisfaction high, but needed more testing before broader deployment. The concept illustrated YouTube's desire to differentiate from old-school TV commercials, giving watchers more control.

By refining these ad placements, YouTube sought a balance that appeased advertisers (who demanded more opportunities) and users (who disliked over-intrusive ads). The varied results underscored the site's iterative approach to generating revenue without alienating the audience.

6.2. Addressing "Advertiser-Friendly" Controversies

As brand safety issues rose, YouTube introduced clearer **advertiser-friendly guidelines**:

1. **Content Limitations**

    - Certain content categories—excessive profanity, graphic violence, sexual content, or discussions of sensitive topics—were flagged as non-advertiser-friendly. Monetization was either disabled or severely limited.

    - This caused friction among creators who tackled serious or controversial subjects. They argued that demonetizing entire topics could discourage meaningful discussions.

2. **Early "Yellow Icons"**
    - In internal systems, YouTube used icons to denote if a video was fully monetized (green) or restricted/demonetized (yellow). A mismatch or sudden yellow icon confused creators who often didn't know why.
    - The appeals process was slow, with mixed results. Some creators felt powerless when their ad revenue vanished overnight due to algorithmic misclassification.
3. **Community Response**
    - While brand safety was a legitimate concern, many longtime YouTubers felt the platform was shifting away from the freewheeling environment they loved. They worried about "corporate sanitization."
    - Nonetheless, YouTube's corporate stance was that consistent brand revenue was crucial for site longevity. Advertiser demands for brand safety left the platform with limited options.

These advertiser-friendly policies exemplified how YouTube's corporate evolution forced it to **codify** content rules for financial stability. Creators navigated a new reality where certain content or language choices might jeopardize monetization.

7. The Internal Struggle: Openness vs. Commercial Viability

7.1. Balancing "Broadcast Yourself" Ethos

YouTube's early motto, "Broadcast Yourself," celebrated **raw, user-driven creativity**. Yet with the influx of:

- High-level corporate deals
- Stricter guidelines

- Complex ad systems

...some staff worried the original spirit was compromised.

1. **Fear of Stifling Innovation**
    - In the push to accommodate large advertisers and big media partners, employees questioned if smaller creators or niche experimentation would get overshadowed.
    - The site tried to reassure staff that user uploads remained the backbone, but official deals and premium content often got front-page features, raising concerns about favoritism.
2. **Auto-Content Filters**
    - Efforts to block copyrighted material or detect hate speech led to false positives. Some comedic or parody videos were taken down or demonetized due to algorithmic errors.
    - This tension highlighted the difficulty of using automated tools for nuanced creative expression. Staff debated how to refine algorithms without undermining user trust.
3. **Community Sentiment**
    - A segment of the community lamented that YouTube felt less like a grassroots playground and more like a "corporate network." They cited official media overshadowing indie channels and heavier rules restricting spontaneity.
    - Others recognized these changes as a necessary step for YouTube's survival at global scale. They argued the site still offered enormous freedom compared to traditional media.

This internal back-and-forth reflected a **philosophical identity crisis**: Could YouTube remain a bastion of user-generated free expression while being a highly regulated, brand-friendly, and globally compliant platform?

7.2. Morale and Identity Among Employees

Amid rapid expansion, employees wrestled with morale issues:

1. **Growing Team Complexity**
    - Project coordination required more meetings, documents, and channels. While many saw it as normal big-company process, ex-startup folks felt it sapped creative spontaneity.

- Some team leads left for smaller startups, missing the adrenaline of early YouTube. Others thrived in the new environment, enjoying stability and career growth.

2. **Internal Communication Gaps**
   - With multiple offices worldwide, miscommunication about feature rollouts or policy changes sometimes occurred. Different time zones and cultural contexts added complexity.
   - Google used internal wikis and email groups, but YouTube staff found it challenging to keep track of every relevant thread or document.

3. **Corporate vs. Startup Mindsets**
   - Some employees who joined post-acquisition came from big tech backgrounds, comfortable with hierarchical structures. Founding-era employees felt overshadowed.
   - Ultimately, managers implemented orientation programs, mentorship, and staff events to unify the workforce, acknowledging that melding two cultures was an ongoing process.

Despite these growing pains, the platform continued to flourish externally. Users rarely saw internal struggles; they simply noticed new features, improved performance, or stricter content enforcement. Inside, YouTube's workforce worked to reconcile past ideals with present realities.

CHAPTER 19: THE TRANSITION INTO MAINSTREAM ENTERTAINMENT

1. Introduction: From Novelty to Everyday Fixture

During its first few years, YouTube was known primarily for short, often amateur videos that circulated virally—funny home clips, comedic sketches, personal vlogs, music covers, and random snippets of everyday life. By around 2008 and 2009, however, the platform's growing **infrastructure, partnerships, and user base** pushed YouTube deeper into the mainstream entertainment world. It was no longer just a website for quirky, user-made content; it was also a place for film promos, TV previews, music videos, and more polished productions.

In this chapter, we explore how YouTube evolved from a niche internet phenomenon into a **mainstream entertainment hub**. We will look at the rise of dedicated brand channels, the platform's collaborations with major production companies, and the ways in which everyday people began to treat YouTube as a default space for discovering news, music, and cultural trends. By the end of this transformation, YouTube was well on its way to **competing** with traditional forms of media, shaping the habits of viewers across the globe.

2. Early Strides Toward Professional Content

2.1. Partnerships with Production Houses

Long before big streaming services dominated, smaller production companies recognized YouTube's potential to **release specialized content**:

1. **Short Web Shows**
    - Some independent studios, seeing how user traction on short videos soared, started producing "web shows"—series of short, scripted episodes designed explicitly for online audiences.
    - While lacking the big budgets of television, these shows often found loyal fans who appreciated direct access, shorter runtimes, and the freedom from strict network censorship.
2. **Experimental Pilots**
    - A few enterprising directors and producers used YouTube as a **testing ground** for new concepts. Releasing a pilot episode for free let them gauge viewer interest. If the show gained traction, they could pitch it to TV networks or sponsors with proof of an existing fan base.

- This approach mirrored the logic of a "minimum viable product": rather than invest heavily in a full season, creators tested their ideas cheaply, letting audience data drive further development.

3. **Quality Upgrades**

   - While early user content was often grainy or unpolished, these production houses brought better cameras, lighting, and scripting. Their content introduced more cinematic visuals to YouTube, helping shift the platform's reputation from purely amateur uploads to a place that could host real storytelling and drama.

   - Some shows integrated with YouTube's interactive features (comments, annotations) to gather feedback, bridging professional-level production with the site's grassroots, participatory ethos.

Although these independent moves didn't instantly overshadow user-generated content, they **planted the seeds** for later expansions of professional material. In the process, they also validated YouTube as a legitimate venue for showcasing higher-quality, serialized entertainment.

2.2. Growth of Official Music Video Presence

Music videos played a major role in YouTube's mainstream shift:

1. **VEVO and Label Collaborations**

   - While VEVO (a joint venture among major labels) did not fully launch until around 2009–2010, the groundwork was laid in this early period. Major labels began systematically uploading music videos to dedicated channels, forging partnerships that allowed them to **monetize** official content rather than fighting endless takedowns.

   - The success of these early uploads—garnering millions of views—proved to labels that YouTube was a key promotional tool. Fans worldwide could instantly see new releases or classic hits, fueling global music discovery.

2. **Tracking Popularity and Hype**

   - Unlike TV music channels (MTV, VH1) with limited slots and scheduled times, YouTube let labels upload music videos whenever they wanted. Artists could promote new singles on social media, linking directly to YouTube, ensuring fans had immediate, around-the-clock access.

   - View counts and comment sections provided near-real-time feedback on which songs resonated, helping labels plan future promotional efforts. This direct listener response upended the older model of relying on radio charts or physical sales data.

3. **User Engagement: Covers and Remixes**

    - With official music videos more accessible, fans continued to post their own covers or remixes, creating a **vibrant** music ecosystem. Official clips inspired user content, which in turn promoted the original songs.

    - Labels began to accept some level of derivative works, occasionally choosing to monetize them via ads rather than forcing removals. This approach kept the fan community engaged, reinforcing YouTube as a central hub for musical creativity.

Hence, the music industry's shift toward official channels and consistent uploads helped normalize YouTube as a primary platform for **entertainment**—especially for younger audiences who were increasingly turning to the internet, not television, to watch new music videos.

3. Brand Channels and Major Advertisers

3.1. Consumer Brands Embrace YouTube

Beyond music and film, large **consumer brands** used YouTube to engage potential customers:

1. **Creative Ad Campaigns**

    - Companies like Old Spice, Coca-Cola, and Nike launched "viral" commercials designed specifically for online sharing, rather than the typical 30-second TV spot.

    - Some of these campaigns encouraged user participation: viewers might remix an ad jingle, create parody responses, or film personal takes on the brand's theme. This interactive dynamic went beyond traditional advertising's one-way approach.

2. **Behind-the-Scenes and Extended Content**

    - A brand channel might post behind-the-scenes clips of upcoming commercials, staff interviews, or "making-of" mini-documentaries. Fans got an inside look at brand creativity, which generated goodwill and curiosity.

    - By offering more than a single ad, companies told deeper brand stories, hoping viewers would form a personal connection. YouTube's unlimited space allowed extra content that would never fit into standard TV ad time.

3. **Contests and Challenges**

    - Brands sometimes ran official challenges—like filming a short comedic video featuring their product—and promised winners a prize or chance to appear in a future commercial. This user-generated approach turned fans into co-creators.

    - The best entries might be featured on the brand's channel, driving engagement and a sense of community ownership around a product or campaign.

These brand experiments made YouTube more than just a place to watch ads: it became a stage for **immersive marketing** that leveraged user interaction. As brands reported success with these experiments, more advertisers flocked to YouTube, fueling the platform's shift into a mainstream promotional powerhouse.

3.2. Sponsorships and Product Placement in User Videos

The rise of **YouTube stars** (see Chapter 16) offered brands new ways to reach audiences:

1. **Direct Sponsorship Deals**

    - Instead of producing their own channel content, some companies paid popular YouTubers to incorporate products into comedic sketches, vlogs, or tutorial videos. This approach felt more organic than a standard commercial.

    - Early brand-creator collaborations were often informal, with limited disclosure guidelines. Nonetheless, they demonstrated the potential for "influencer marketing"—long before it became the buzzword it is today.

2. **Customized Product Integrations**

    - A comedic channel might revolve an entire skit around a brand, delivering comedic references that felt more entertaining than a forced pitch. Or a beauty vlogger might showcase certain cosmetics in a "get ready with me" routine.

    - These integrated approaches made ads less intrusive, as viewers saw them as part of the normal content. Companies recognized the advantage of tapping into a creator's authentic style.

3. **Fan Reactions**

    - Some viewers objected if sponsorship felt excessive or dishonest—especially if creators never mentioned they were paid. Others found it acceptable when disclosed properly, appreciating that sponsorships helped creators fund more ambitious content.

- Over time, this sponsorship model expanded, reinforcing YouTube's role as a **mainstream marketing channel**. The same approach that once fueled brand tie-ins on TV now flourished in a more personal, interactive format.

Overall, the infiltration of major brands into user-generated content blurred boundaries. YouTube emerged as a space where everyday personalities could produce content on par with mainstream commercials, and advertisers recognized the platform's unique blend of authenticity, scale, and immediate audience feedback.

4. Recognition and Credibility in the Public Eye

4.1. Coverage in Mainstream News

By 2008–2009, YouTube was routinely referenced in **major news outlets**:

1. **Discussion of Viral Hits**
    - Network morning shows often ran segments like "What's Trending on YouTube This Week?" featuring a short montage of viral clips. This re-introduced broadcast viewers—who might not be avid internet users—to top online sensations.
    - This exposure fed a cycle: a clip went viral on YouTube, mainstream news covered it, then more viewers rushed to YouTube to watch, further boosting its popularity.
2. **Serious Journalism**
    - Beyond funny videos, news programs highlighted significant user footage of current events—a protest, disaster, or on-the-ground report from conflict zones. This elevated YouTube's reputation as a "citizen journalism" hub.
    - Commentators debated how the platform democratized news coverage. Traditional broadcasters recognized that YouTube could scoop them by airing raw eyewitness clips before a news truck even arrived.
3. **End-of-Year Roundups**
    - Television specials or newspaper features enumerated "Top YouTube Moments" of the year. This gave the platform an air of **cultural permanence**, showing it was no longer a passing fad but integral to contemporary media coverage.

As mainstream coverage normalized YouTube, the public began to see it less as a curious website for random uploads and more as a **trusted source** of entertainment, information, and cultural trends.

4.2. Celebrity Appearances and Mentions

Celebrities from film, music, and sports referenced YouTube in interviews:

1. **Actors and Musicians**
    - On talk shows, celebrities frequently mentioned "Did you see that on YouTube?" or "My kids showed me this on YouTube," underscoring how the platform permeated daily entertainment habits.
    - Some stars admitted discovering new talents, comedic sketches, or lesser-known songs on the platform, giving it an aura of authority in uncovering fresh creativity.
2. **Award Ceremonies**
    - Early YouTubers occasionally received nods at digital media awards or were invited as presenters at mainstream award shows, bridging the gap between web content and old-school ceremonies.
    - Although not as common as in later years, these cameo appearances validated the idea that success on YouTube could translate into broader cultural recognition.
3. **Cross-Promotion**
    - Film stars posted "thank you" videos on YouTube after receiving major accolades, using the platform to address fans directly, bypassing traditional press statements. This personal approach endeared them to online audiences.
    - Some television series had cast members produce comedic behind-the-scenes clips specifically for YouTube, building hype for the show.

In short, mentions of YouTube in celebrity interviews or mainstream awards contributed to the platform's acceptance as a standard part of modern entertainment. It was no longer unusual for a star to mention YouTube promotions or references—these gestures affirmed YouTube's mainstream foothold.

5. YouTube Live and High-Profile Events

5.1. The First YouTube Live Events

Around 2008, YouTube began exploring **live streaming**, starting with special events:

1. **YouTube Live (2008)**
   - In November 2008, YouTube hosted a large-scale live broadcast called "YouTube Live," featuring performances by popular creators, musicians, and comedians. This San Francisco event was an effort to bring the online community together in a physical show, simultaneously streamed worldwide.
   - Acts ranged from famous YouTubers like the band "Chester See," "Bo Burnham," or comedic personalities, to mainstream musicians who recognized the potential audience. Fans could tune in live, experience the show's energy, and chat online in real time.
2. **Experimenting with Live Technology**
   - Streaming a major event to millions challenged YouTube's servers. The platform tested new protocols to handle high-traffic concurrency. Though some viewers experienced buffering, it proved YouTube's ambition to compete with television broadcasts.
   - This milestone hinted at a future where YouTube might host sports, concerts, or major announcements in real time—like a TV network.
3. **Reception and Legacy**
   - While the production felt experimental, fans appreciated seeing their favorite online stars share a stage, legitimizing the "YouTuber" identity. Traditional outlets covered the event, noting its unique mix of internet-born and mainstream talents.
   - Although subsequent "YouTube Live" shows in that exact format didn't occur immediately, the concept of large live events on the platform laid groundwork for future expansions into live streaming, eventually used for gaming, e-sports, and real-time cultural events.

These early live efforts demonstrated that YouTube sought to be more than a clip library—it aimed to be a **real-time entertainment platform** capable of hosting big, immediate spectacles, akin to a TV network's live special.

5.2. Partnerships for Global-Scale Events

YouTube also eyed partnerships to stream or highlight major global happenings:

1. **Concerts and Music Festivals**

    - Some music festivals tested short live broadcasts on YouTube, giving viewers worldwide a taste of the performances. Though schedules were limited, the potential for a virtual audience of millions was alluring.

    - This preceded the era of large-scale festival streaming but showed that digital broadcasting could expand a concert's reach far beyond local attendees.

2. **Political and Cultural Events**

    - During major political occasions—like presidential debates or candidate forums—YouTube collaborated with news networks (Chapter 12) to co-stream segments or host user-submitted questions.

    - Cultural events such as New Year's Eve celebrations in big cities occasionally integrated YouTube streams for global viewers who couldn't watch on cable channels.

3. **Technical Challenges**

    - Scaling a live broadcast to hundreds of thousands (or millions) of concurrent viewers tested the platform's backbone. At times, these streams had to be regionally distributed to avoid lag.

    - The site's experience with on-demand content was robust, but live events demanded new approaches to buffering, real-time chat moderation, and failover systems.

By experimenting with these large-scale events, YouTube stepped closer to mainstream broadcast territory, where coverage of big cultural moments had long been a hallmark of television. Each success fueled user expectations that **anything** might eventually appear on YouTube in real time.

6. YouTube's Growing Role in Public Discourse

6.1. Political Debates and Global Dialogues

We've previously discussed YouTube's part in the **2008 U.S. elections**. By 2009, the platform's influence on broader public discourse had expanded:

1. **Town Halls and Q&A Sessions**
   - Some political figures, beyond U.S. presidential candidates, used YouTube to conduct Q&A videos. Citizens submitted questions in comment sections or via video responses.
   - This direct engagement bypassed traditional press conferences, letting officials speak to voters unfiltered. While not universal, it signaled the rising acceptance of YouTube as a channel for official communication.
2. **NGOs and Humanitarian Causes**
   - Non-governmental organizations discovered YouTube could highlight urgent issues—disaster relief, environmental advocacy, human rights campaigns—using powerful visuals to mobilize public support.
   - Users often responded by donating money or volunteering after seeing heartfelt appeals, showcasing how mainstream YouTube was for activism and awareness-raising.
3. **International Perspectives**
   - People across different countries posted personal testimonies about local events or social movements. News outlets or global audiences used YouTube to glean first-hand glimpses, sometimes circumventing censored state media.
   - Governments kept a close watch, aware that YouTube gave dissidents or minority voices a public platform. This occasionally led to partial blocks or pressure on YouTube to remove politically sensitive material (as covered in Chapter 18).

YouTube's function as a **public forum** for political, social, and humanitarian issues further solidified its mainstream relevance. It wasn't just comedic or musical content capturing headlines; YouTube was also shaping how society debated pressing matters.

6.2. Educational and Informational Channels

A quieter but significant area of growth was **educational content**:

1. **Academic Lectures and Tutorials**
    - Universities and teachers started uploading lectures, language lessons, and tutorial videos, which gave students and self-learners free access to knowledge.
    - Channels like "Khan Academy" (founded in 2006 but growing rapidly around 2008–2009) exemplified how YouTube could deliver math, science, or history lessons to millions. This signaled a shift from pure entertainment to **edutainment**.
2. **DIY and How-To**
    - Another trend was practical "how-to" videos—cooking tutorials, home repair guides, coding lessons, gardening tips, and more. Traditional how-to books or manuals felt slow compared to an immediate demonstration on YouTube.
    - Viewers could pause, rewind, and follow step by step, prompting an ongoing wave of tutorial creators who gained substantial followings.
3. **Cultural Acceptance of Online Learning**
    - As these channels grew, mainstream media and educational institutions acknowledged that YouTube was a valid resource for informal learning. TV documentaries or newspapers occasionally cited popular how-to channels as references for everyday tasks.
    - While some worried about misinformation or unverified sources, the best educational channels built reputations for quality, encouraging a new era of open, accessible knowledge-sharing.

Educational and informational content deepened YouTube's **mainstream integration** by appealing to those uninterested in memes or pop culture. The platform was no longer purely about entertainment; it also served as a vast library of practical and academic resources, further embedding itself into daily life.

7. Viewing Habits and Pop Culture Phenomena

7.1. Shifting Television Audiences

As YouTube grew, many younger viewers spent more time watching videos online than on traditional TV:

1. **Cord-Cutting Precursors**

    - The term "cord-cutting" would become common in the 2010s, but even in 2008–2009, TV viewership patterns were starting to shift. People realized they could find highlights, comedic bits, or music videos on YouTube **on demand**, avoiding scheduled broadcasts.

    - This "shift in eyeballs" worried TV networks, prompting them to rush new strategies—streaming episodes on official websites, licensing content to digital platforms, or forging deeper YouTube partnerships.

2. **User-Controlled Playlists**

    - YouTube introduced or refined playlist features, letting viewers queue up multiple clips or watch entire series of short episodes seamlessly. This user-curated "channel" approach appealed to those who disliked passive channel surfing on TV.

    - The sense of personal curation empowered viewers: they picked exactly what they wanted to see, no filler or schedules to endure.

3. **Social Sharing**

    - Sharing a YouTube link via email or early social media (e.g., Facebook, MySpace) became an everyday act. This created micro-communities around specific videos, fostering group watching experiences that TV often lacked unless everyone watched simultaneously.

    - Viral videos gave friends something to discuss at school or work the next day, just as people once talked about a TV show's big twist. The difference was that "everyone could watch it whenever they wanted" rather than being tied to a broadcast time.

Hence, by 2009, it was evident that **entertainment consumption** was increasingly on viewers' terms. YouTube exemplified that shift, normalizing the idea of a decentralized, user-curated experience that traditional channels struggled to replicate.

7.2. Meme Culture and Shared References

YouTube's role in **meme culture** underlined its influence on everyday conversation:

1. **Instant Cultural Touchstones**
    - Viral hits like "Charlie Bit My Finger" or comedic music parodies became references people casually dropped in offline chats. Even those who didn't actively browse YouTube heard about these hits through mainstream coverage.
    - Memes that originated on YouTube often found their way to T-shirts, late-night jokes, or even cameo references in commercials or TV sitcoms.
2. **Mashups and Parodies**
    - The platform's user-friendly environment for uploading "response" clips fueled comedic parodies or mashups, in which fans reworked popular elements. These spinoffs extended a meme's lifespan, making it even more entrenched in cultural discourse.
    - Traditional media sometimes struggled to keep pace with meme cycles, which could evolve at lightning speed. YouTube served as ground zero for short-lived yet explosive phenomena, bridging different segments of popular culture.
3. **Cross-Border Resonance**
    - The global nature of YouTube meant a silly comedic video from one country could spark interest worldwide, bridging language gaps with slapstick humor or striking visuals.
    - This global meme explosion illustrated how the site bypassed local broadcast restrictions, making comedic or emotional content accessible to anyone with an internet connection.

In these ways, YouTube became a platform where **pop culture** was generated, not just distributed—a fundamental shift from the one-to-many broadcast model of traditional entertainment.

8. The Path Toward Future Streaming Dominance

8.1. Seeds of Original Programming

Although not fully realized by 2009, YouTube's flirtation with professional web series hinted at a future where it might **commission or fund original content**:

1. **Early Mini-Grants**

    - A few top creators or small production outfits reported receiving small financial support from YouTube for special projects. Though unpublicized, these micro-grants allowed some channels to produce more ambitious short films.

    - While not a formal "YouTube Originals" program at that time, it showed the platform's willingness to invest beyond ad revenue splits.

2. **Premium Content Discussions**

    - Internal brainstorming at YouTube and Google touched on whether a subscription model or pay-per-view approach could support feature-length films or exclusive series. The idea was met with caution—YouTube's identity revolved around free access.

    - Nonetheless, these early talks planted the notion that YouTube might one day host full-fledged premium shows, especially if competitor platforms arose.

3. **Experiments with Movie Rentals**

    - Around 2009, YouTube quietly tested a movie rental service with limited titles, mostly indie films or festival features. This was a small-scale pilot, overshadowed by user-generated content, but it represented a step toward future streaming potentials.

Though these experiments were modest, they foreshadowed the massive expansions in the next decade, when YouTube would face competition from Netflix, Amazon, Hulu, and more. At the tail end of the 2000s, YouTube was already **probing** how to leverage its popularity for more structured, high-end entertainment offerings.

8.2. Competitors and Market Response

YouTube's mainstream success motivated **rival platforms** to emerge or reinvent themselves:

1. **Dailymotion, Vimeo, and Others**

    - Although these sites existed from YouTube's early days (Chapter 9), some sought a unique niche. Vimeo, for instance, emphasized artistic and high-quality uploads, attracting filmmakers or design-focused creators.

    - Dailymotion targeted specific international audiences and formed partnerships with certain media. However, none matched YouTube's scale or brand recognition.

2. **Facebook's Video Aspirations**

    - While Facebook at the time was mostly about status updates and photos, it began exploring video features, letting users post short clips on profiles. This was more social than broadcast, but signaled possible future competition for user attention.

    - The question loomed: would people prefer specialized video platforms like YouTube, or a multi-purpose social network that also supported video?

3. **Market Consolidation**

    - Smaller video-sharing start-ups struggled to compete with YouTube's user base, technology, and backing from Google. Many pivoted or closed.

    - Traditional media networks that once toyed with launching their own video sites realized it was easier to partner with YouTube than build a new platform from scratch.

Hence, by 2009, YouTube appeared poised to maintain its **dominant** position in online video. It was the go-to site for user uploads, music videos, brand marketing, budding web series, and all manner of viral phenomena. Its mainstream infiltration made it tough for challengers to catch up.

CHAPTER 20: LEGACY OF THE EARLY YOUTUBE ERA

1. Introduction: Reflecting on a Transformative Platform

From its launch in 2005 through the late 2000s, YouTube underwent a meteoric rise, radically altering how we share, consume, and produce videos. It began as a simple idea among three former PayPal employees to solve the problem of uploading and viewing user-generated clips online. In just a few years, the platform evolved into a **global phenomenon**, simultaneously challenging and collaborating with traditional media. Along the way, it nurtured entirely new forms of digital celebrity, pioneered interactive advertising strategies, and popularized on-demand video culture for a global audience.

This final chapter takes a broad look back at YouTube's **early legacy**—the key lessons, lasting impacts, and unresolved questions from the site's first transformative years. We'll consider how YouTube changed entertainment, empowered content creators, reshaped notions of free expression, and laid the groundwork for a new era of streaming, social media, and online culture that we continue to experience today. Though subsequent developments would further refine YouTube's role, it is the **foundation** established in these early years that made everything else possible.

2. Key Innovations and Their Lasting Influence

2.1. User-Generated Content as Mainstream

Before YouTube, most online video platforms were niche or cumbersome, requiring specific players or limited by bandwidth constraints. YouTube's **easy upload** process and in-browser playback changed the game:

1. **Democratization of Video**
    - Anyone with a camera and internet access could share clips instantly. This democratization created an enormous ecosystem of amateur creators who felt empowered to publish content that would never have reached a national audience on TV.
    - The idea of "broadcasting yourself" paved the way for the influencer culture that would proliferate across the internet. Even outside YouTube, social platforms adapted a model that encouraged user creation and sharing.
2. **Viral Mechanics**
    - YouTube's embedding feature and simple share links let videos travel across blogs, social media profiles, and email chains. Viral hits no longer depended on TV show spotlights; they could spread organically user-to-user.
    - This viral phenomenon influenced how advertisers, musicians, and politicians approached outreach, understanding that **grassroots excitement** often outperformed top-down marketing.
3. **Shifting Content Standards**
    - Traditional television had set "quality" expectations—polished editing, professional sets, big budgets. YouTube showed that raw, authentic, or comedic bedroom recordings could attract millions of viewers.
    - Over time, mainstream media adopted more informal, personal content styles, reflecting the authenticity that made YouTube so popular.

By legitimizing user-generated content on a massive scale, YouTube influenced nearly every social platform that followed, setting the tone for a participatory internet culture where **every user** is a potential creator.

2.2. The Rise of Short-Form and On-Demand Viewing

Early YouTube popularized the idea that short, on-demand clips could be just as compelling as scheduled TV:

1. **Attention Economy**
   - The site's short video lengths suited modern, hectic lifestyles, letting people watch multiple random clips in quick bursts. This convenience affected everything from comedic timing to how we engage with news or music videos.
   - Audiences grew to expect entertainment in easily digestible segments, fueling the later success of platforms focusing on ultra-short content.
2. **Decline of Appointment Viewing**
   - While TV networks clung to scheduled programming, YouTube normalized the idea that viewers watch what they want, whenever they want—be it a funny sketch, a music video, or a tutorial.
   - This contributed to the broader shift toward DVRs, streaming services, and on-demand platforms, ultimately challenging the primacy of linear TV schedules.
3. **Recommendation-Driven Exploration**
   - YouTube's "related videos" and basic recommendation algorithms shaped how viewers discovered new content. This "rabbit hole" browsing changed viewing habits, as people spent hours following suggested links.
   - Future streaming services expanded on this concept with more advanced personalization, but YouTube pioneered a user-centric discovery process that steered people toward diverse videos in real time.

Hence, the platform's focus on quick, anytime clips opened cultural space for personalized, flexible viewing, forming the basis of the modern digital entertainment economy.

3. Transformation of Celebrity and Creator Economies

3.1. Self-Made Stars and Influencer Marketing

YouTube's early Partner Program (Chapter 15) and supportive community environment led to **unprecedented** transformations in how entertainers and personalities emerged:

1. **Dismantling Gatekeepers**

    - Traditional routes to fame (Hollywood auditions, label signings, TV scouting) were bypassed by charismatic YouTubers who built massive followings from bedrooms or small studios.

    - This phenomenon inspired countless creators worldwide, showing that raw talent and online savvy could generate success without institutional approval.

2. **Closer Fan Relationships**

    - YouTubers interacted directly with comments, Q&A videos, and social media, forging deeper emotional bonds than typical celebrities had. Fans felt personally connected, forming communities around channels rather than just passively watching.

    - This approach presaged the modern influencer model, where authenticity and personal connection often trump polished or traditional star power.

3. **Sponsored Content Foundations**

    - Brand partnerships and product placements within YouTube videos marked the earliest large-scale influencer marketing. While not always clearly disclosed, these deals sparked the concept of leveraging personal channels for brand promotion.

    - Today's influencer-driven advertising ecosystem, seen on Instagram, TikTok, and beyond, owes much to the initial brand-creator deals on YouTube.

Thus, YouTube played a pivotal role in **reshaping the entertainment talent pipeline**, making it more merit-based, user-driven, and interactive.

3.2. Creator-Platform Dynamics

The relationships between creators and the platform itself evolved significantly:

1. **Monetization and Incentives**

    - YouTube's revenue-sharing model introduced the idea that "ordinary people" could earn real income from online videos. This concept democratized creative entrepreneurship, attracting more talents to digital production.

- Over time, disputes over algorithm changes, demonetization, and brand safety guidelines revealed the **fragility** of relying on a platform's policies for income. This foreshadowed modern debates about platform dependence among influencers.

2. **Community Building**

    - The site's early emphasis on comments, video responses, and collaboration fueled a sense of camaraderie among creators. They shared tips, cross-promoted channels, and formed niche communities for comedy, vlogging, music, and more.

    - As user bases expanded, these communities faced challenges—trolls, stricter guidelines, brand intrusion—but the fundamental community ethos remained a defining characteristic.

3. **Career Launchpad**

    - Several YouTube personalities transitioned to mainstream media (TV roles, record deals, movie cameos) or built full-fledged businesses (merchandising, tours).

    - Even those who didn't cross over found lasting success within the YouTube ecosystem, forging careers unimaginable before 2005. Creators from diverse backgrounds—housewives, gamers, teachers—demonstrated how the platform's early era truly opened new career paths.

In short, YouTube's first few years set the template for modern content creation economies, showing how platforms and users can collaborate—albeit amid tension—to build lucrative, community-driven digital ecosystems.

4. Media Industry Evolution in Response

4.1. Traditional Media's Shift to Online Integration

We have seen how TV, film, and music industries initially resisted YouTube before recognizing its value. Over time, that partial acceptance grew into a broader **online-first** mindset:

1. **Multiplatform Releases**

    - Major networks tested simultaneous or next-day streaming releases, acknowledging that loyal fans might watch on official websites or YouTube channels. While not fully replacing broadcast, this signaled a pivot to adapt to on-demand habits.

- Film studios placed greater emphasis on YouTube trailers to build hype. The old system of exclusive trailer premieres in theaters or on TV was no longer enough; YouTube views became a critical metric of a movie's buzz.

2. **Adaptation of Online Metrics**
   - Traditional media used YouTube analytics—view counts, likes, watch time—to gauge public interest in show segments or new acts. This real-time feedback loop was a stark contrast to slower TV ratings or box-office tallies.
   - The success of certain online campaigns or short web shows sometimes prompted TV networks to pick them up, reversing the old model where networks discovered talent strictly through agent pitches.
3. **Industry Restructuring**
   - Realizing the power of user-driven distribution, entertainment conglomerates established in-house digital divisions dedicated to maximizing YouTube presence, influencer collaborations, and official digital releases.
   - Although tensions over copyright persisted, the general trend leaned toward synergy—merging YouTube's vast audience with the polished content of legacy media.

By responding to YouTube's success, mainstream media laid groundwork for broader streaming expansions, eventually giving rise to entire direct-to-consumer platforms. YouTube's early success effectively **pushed** traditional entertainment to modernize its distribution and promotional strategies.

4.2. Shaping Future Streaming Landscape

The wave of streaming services that emerged in the 2010s—Netflix, Hulu, Amazon Prime Video—took cues from YouTube's demonstration that viewers wanted on-demand content accessible anytime:

1. **Viewer Autonomy**
   - YouTube illustrated that user-driven choice and flexible, ad-supported models could work at scale. Although Netflix adopted a subscription approach, the fundamental principle of letting viewers pick what to watch at any moment was validated by YouTube's success.
   - Other services realized that robust recommendation systems, user profiles, and instant streaming were essential components to keep audiences engaged.

2. **Advertising Evolution**

    - The multi-format ad system YouTube developed—pre-roll, overlays, mid-roll—became standard references for streaming sites with free or freemium tiers.
    - Over time, other platforms refined user data to further personalize ads, building on Google/YouTube's early experiments with targeted advertising.

3. **Original Content Paradigm**

    - As we saw in Chapter 19, YouTube's flirtation with original mini-series hinted that streaming-first shows could succeed. Netflix and others fully embraced the potential of original programming, but YouTube's early notion of direct distribution to fans was a key inspiration.
    - Even if YouTube didn't become the biggest player in original scripted series, the concept that an online platform could directly fund and distribute premium shows was partly validated by YouTube's first steps.

Hence, while YouTube stayed primarily user-focused, its pioneering efforts in on-demand access, ad formats, and even early glimpses of original shows played a crucial role in shaping the broader streaming revolution that followed.

5. Cultural Shifts and Social Impact

5.1. Global Community and Cross-Cultural Exchange

YouTube's accessibility across borders broadened cultural exchange:

1. **New Windows into Other Societies**

    - Instead of official documentaries, everyday people uploaded local festivals, daily routines, or personal commentaries. Viewers worldwide peeked into lives they'd never see on mainstream TV.
    - This built empathy and curiosity across cultures, occasionally sparking viral connections that transcended language barriers.

2. **Language Adaptations**

    - As covered in Chapter 13, YouTube localized interfaces, spurring growth in non-English content. Creators from various countries found local audiences but sometimes reached unexpected foreign fans too.

- This global mixing advanced the idea that **anyone** could find an audience, no matter their location or native tongue—contributing to a sense of shared global community.

3. **Political and Social Awareness**

   - Activists worldwide used YouTube to highlight injustices, protest movements, or environmental concerns. The site's open platform amplified voices typically overlooked by major media outlets.

   - Though tensions with governments and censorship issues persisted, the early era proved YouTube could function as an influential channel for grassroots awareness campaigns, reshaping how society engaged with social and political topics.

This global dimension set YouTube apart from older forms of entertainment distribution, bridging geographical divides and forging a more interconnected cultural landscape.

5.2. Shaping Digital Communication Norms

YouTube's comment culture and content-sharing habits influenced broader **online communication**:

1. **Visual Expression**

   - People became accustomed to expressing reactions through video responses, quick comedic references, or personal "rants" on camera. This visual emphasis paved the way for the next generation of platforms like TikTok or Instagram Reels, which revolve around short-form, personality-driven videos.

   - Memes, comedic bits, and personal diaries turned into standard ways to communicate ideas or jokes online.

2. **Interactive Feedback**

   - The notion of immediate feedback—comments, likes, ratings—encouraged more engaged audiences who expected the same interactivity across social media.

   - The concept of "subscribing" to an individual's content also became ubiquitous on the internet, shaping how we follow influencers, newsletters, or podcasts across platforms.

3. **Community Moderation**

    ◦ The challenges YouTube faced with trolls, harassment, or hateful content set precedents for how other sites approached moderation. People realized that open comment sections could spawn both vibrant dialogues and toxic behavior.

    ◦ Subsequent communities and platforms learned from YouTube's early stumbles, implementing more nuanced moderation tools or adopting stricter user guidelines from the outset.

Hence, the early YouTube era seeded practices—subscribing, liking, commenting—that became standard features of modern digital interaction, altering how billions of people create and consume content online.

6. Lessons, Hurdles, and Unresolved Questions

6.1. Balancing Openness with Responsibility

YouTube's growth highlighted the tension between **free expression** and necessary oversight:

1. **Upholding Freedom of Content**

    ◦ The site's success stemmed from minimal upload barriers, letting creativity flourish. Yet this openness also invited problematic content (violence, hate speech, explicit material).

    ◦ Stricter guidelines were inevitable, but they prompted debates about censorship, fairness, and the risk of punishing harmless creators by accident.

2. **Algorithmic Challenges**

    ◦ Early recommendation algorithms, while driving user engagement, sometimes propelled extremist or misleading videos. Though less scrutinized in the late 2000s, the seeds of future controversies were evident.

    ◦ The question of how to responsibly nudge user attention remained complex, as the platform's fundamental model thrived on watch-time and clickthrough rates.

3. **Platform Liability**

    ◦ The DMCA safe harbor concept shielded YouTube from direct liability for user uploads if it acted promptly on takedown notices. This legal structure was crucial for the platform's viability.

- Still, critics contended that large platforms must take more proactive measures, a conversation that would intensify in subsequent years.

Balancing these concerns remained a **core challenge** from YouTube's earliest successes—one that would only become more complicated as the platform scaled and public scrutiny intensified.

6.2. Creator Monetization vs. Corporate Needs

Creators benefited from YouTube's ad revenue, yet controversies around demonetization and brand safety signaled deeper **structural tensions**:

1. **Algorithmic Dependence**
    - With the site's commercial success came increasingly complex algorithmic curation and monetization decisions. Creators who thrived under one algorithm update sometimes struggled under the next.
    - This precarious reliance on a single platform's policies foreshadowed the modern "creator economy," in which abrupt platform changes can upend livelihoods overnight.
2. **Quality vs. Commercial Viability**
    - Many creators wanted freedom to address controversial or mature topics. Brand-friendly guidelines, however, often penalized them financially.
    - The platform's attempt to attract big advertisers while maintaining a diverse content library proved an ongoing tightrope act, never fully resolved in the early era.
3. **Creator Autonomy**
    - Even as some creators enjoyed fame and income, they faced demands to produce content more frequently or shape content according to platform-friendly or advertiser-friendly norms. The question arose: does corporate involvement stifle the platform's original spirit of personal expression?
    - The early era ended with that tension still in flux—YouTube wanted to remain open and user-driven, yet also needed consistent brand revenue to support ever-growing bandwidth and staffing costs.

In sum, the friction between "independent creator culture" and "corporate monetization imperatives" became deeply ingrained in YouTube's DNA, shaping its evolution and how future platforms would tackle similar dilemmas.

7. The Legacy Moving Forward

7.1. YouTube as a Cultural Archive

One lasting legacy of early YouTube is its role as a **cultural time capsule**:

1. **Preserving Early Viral Moments**
   - Iconic videos from the 2005–2009 period remain part of internet folklore, often studied or referenced as the origin of modern meme culture.
   - Even personal vlogs from that era serve as historical snapshots of everyday life before smartphones and streaming services became omnipresent.
2. **Record of Shifting Entertainment**
   - YouTube's library documents how comedic styles, video quality, and audience interactions changed over time. Researchers and pop-culture historians see it as a living archive of evolving tastes.
   - This open repository of user uploads captures social trends, fashion, technology, and political sentiments in raw form, unfiltered by institutional gatekeepers.
3. **Ongoing Acccssibility**
   - Videos posted a decade or more ago often remain online, accessible to new viewers. This contrasts with ephemeral TV reruns or physically decaying media, reinforcing YouTube's unique archiving function.

Thus, beyond entertainment or marketing, YouTube's early library collectively stands as an ongoing public resource, bridging historical events, personal stories, and cultural shifts in an enduring digital format.

7.2. Continuation of "Broadcast Yourself" in a Corporate Context

While corporate transformations steered YouTube toward brand safety and official content, the platform **never fully lost** its user-generated core:

1. **Evolution Not Replacement**
   - Even as professional channels and media partnerships grew, user uploads still comprised the majority of new videos. Countless niches—beauty tips, gaming

highlights, science demos—flourished, reflecting the original "Broadcast Yourself" ethos.

  - Corporate and user content coexisted, shaping a hybrid environment. This mix remains a cornerstone of YouTube's identity, though each major policy shift can tilt the balance.

2. **Ripple Effect on Future Platforms**
   - YouTube's success validated the belief that an open platform for user videos could flourish. Platforms like Vine (later replaced by TikTok) adopted a shorter-video approach, while Instagram and Snapchat integrated video features, all borrowing from YouTube's user-driven concept.
   - The notion that everyday creators can produce influential content remains a central premise of the modern social media landscape, echoing the intangible power of "Broadcast Yourself."

3. **Public Expectation**
   - People now anticipate that any major event, comedic moment, or personal milestone might appear on YouTube. They also expect site features—playlists, likes, comments, subscriptions—as standard in any new video app.
   - This baseline of user-friendly, open-access, interactive video is perhaps the most universal legacy of YouTube's early period.

Despite shifts in monetization, curation, or corporate oversight, the principle of everyday expression on a global scale remains **enduring**—a testament to those early years when YouTube prioritized user creativity and communal engagement.

8. Conclusion of Chapter 20

Reflecting on YouTube's early years reveals a story of **dramatic change** in the worlds of entertainment, media distribution, and internet culture. Starting as a solution to the problem of easily sharing personal video clips, YouTube rapidly scaled into a global platform that:

- **Empowered** a generation of self-made creators and personalities, allowing them to earn audiences and incomes without legacy media gatekeepers.
- **Redefined** how viewers consume video, popularizing short-form, on-demand, and algorithm-driven discovery methods that continue to shape the broader streaming landscape.

- **Catalyzed** major transformations in advertising, music promotion, film distribution, and television programming, forcing traditional media to adapt or risk irrelevance.

- **Balanced** (sometimes uneasily) the ideals of open expression with commercial necessities, user moderation, and legal obligations—an ongoing struggle that shaped its evolution and remains relevant today.

By 2009, YouTube was no longer merely a start-up phenomenon but a **cornerstone** of global internet usage. Its legacy can be seen in how we engage with content, how we define and celebrate new forms of celebrity, and how we utilize video for everything from activism to education. Many of the platform's biggest challenges—copyright, moderation, brand safety—found their roots in these foundational years, and the platform's handling of them set a precedent for the digital age to come.

While subsequent developments (beyond this book's historical scope) further refined and complicated YouTube's place in the world, these early chapters remain the **blueprint** for how a small video-sharing idea can revolutionize global media. The lessons of community-building, easy sharing, direct fan engagement, and open upload policies continue to reverberate across the internet. And so, as we conclude this account of YouTube's formative era, we recognize it as one of the pivotal innovations in modern history—forever changing the way we create, watch, and share video in a digitally connected world.

Help Us Share Your Thoughts!

Dear reader,

Thank you for spending your time with this book. We hope it brought you enjoyment and a few new ideas to think about. If there was anything that didn't work for you, or if you have suggestions on how we can improve, please let us know at **kontakt@skriuwer.com**. Your feedback means a lot to us and helps us make our books even better.

If you enjoyed this book, we would be very grateful if you left a review on the site where you purchased it. Your review not only helps other readers find our books, but also encourages us to keep creating more stories and materials that you'll love.

By choosing Skriuwer, you're also supporting **Frisian**—a minority language mainly spoken in the northern Netherlands. Although **Frisian** has a rich history, the number of speakers is shrinking, and it's at risk of dying out. Your purchase helps fund resources to preserve and promote this language, such as educational programs and learning tools. If you'd like to learn more about Frisian or even start learning it yourself, please visit **www.learnfrisian.com**.

Thank you for being part of our community. We look forward to sharing more books with you in the future.

Warm regards,
The Skriuwer

www.ingramcontent.com/pod-product-compliance
Lightning Source LLC
Chambersburg PA
CBHW050526240926
51846CB00003B/713
* 9 7 8 3 5 6 5 0 8 1 2 8 8 *